ANTI-STRESS
PUZZLES

Dr Gareth Moore is the author of a wide range of brain-training and puzzle books for both children and adults, including *Clever Commuter*, *Fast Brain Workouts*, *Brain Games for Clever Kids* and many other titles.

He created the daily brain-training site **Brained Up**, www.brainedup.com, and runs the puzzle website PuzzleMix.com. He gained his Ph.D from Cambridge University (UK) in the field of Machine Learning, and has contributed to various advanced projects for leading technology companies.

ANTI-STRESS
PUZZLES

DR GARETH MOORE

Michael O'Mara Books Limited

First published in Great Britain in 2015 by
Michael O'Mara Books Limited
9 Lion Yard
Tremadoc Road
London SW4 7NQ

Originally published in 2006 under the title 'The 10-Minute Brain Workout'.

A CIP catalogue record for this book is available from
the British Library.

Papers used by Michael O'Mara Books Limited are natural, recyclable products made from wood grown in sustainable forests. The manufacturing processes conform to the environmental regulations of the country of origin.

ISBN: 978-1-78243-474-0 in paperback print format

1 2 3 4 5 6 7 8 9 10

www.mombooks.com

Designed and typeset by Gareth Moore

Printed and bound in Great Britain by CPI Group (UK) Ltd,
Croydon, CR0 4YY

CONTENTS

INTRODUCTION

Anti-stress Puzzles

Step back from the stresses of everyday life with this book of brain-training puzzles and exercises, and let the tensions of the real world drift away as you try the tasks on these pages. They'll even help you keep your most important organ – your brain – in tip-top working order. As your brain begins to think in different ways, you may also find yourself thinking up new solutions to real-life problems you have.

Challenge and Reward

Each self-contained exercise is designed to both challenge and reward, providing a sense of achievement on completion.

There are three skill levels in this book: beginner, advanced and expert. As you progress, the tasks will become trickier. This continued challenge is an important part of the subsequent sense of achievement you will feel for successfully completing a puzzle, which may also help alleviate stress. A continued challenge is also a key requirement for any brain-training task. If, however, you find any puzzle starting to become stressful to solve, or simply aren't having fun, then you should turn to the solutions for some help. The solution to any puzzle is always on the page immediately following the exercise, and you could for example add an extra clue to a Sudoku, or work backwards from a given answer to reason out why it is correct.

Mental and Physical Exercise

Just as physical exercise is important for maintaining general health and well-being, mental exercise is equally important for maintaining our brains. Exercising your body on a regular basis improves muscle tone, increasing the flow of blood and so improving the delivery of oxygen and nutrients to your muscles. Similarly, your brain also benefits from regular exercise, allowing you to think in new ways and with greater speed. Exercising your brain is as easy as keeping it learning with novel tasks and challenges, which is why this book consists of 90 varied exercises that will help you build up your brain to keep it fit and healthy. And what's more you should have fun, and become less stressed, as you do so!

Different types of mental challenge work different parts of your brain, just as different types of exercise work different muscles in your body. At a gym you can choose from a range of exercise machines and weights programmes that are designed to target specific muscle groups, or alternatively you can go swimming or join an aerobics class where you will be exercising many more muscles for a much more comprehensive workout. Research has shown that in this respect the brain is remarkably similar. Focusing on a single problem or task for a lengthy period of time tends to use only a small part of the brain, while working through a series of shorter but more varied tasks uses much more of it. That's where *Anti-stress Puzzles* comes in – it's packed full of a mix of different puzzles, challenges, observation and memory tests. Each page has a task or set of tasks that should take you no more than ten or so minutes, but will quite possibly contribute more to your general mental well-being than a whole day of focusing on a single problem.

But why should we make an effort to make better use of our brains if we don't absolutely have to? Again, you can compare using more of your brain to using more of your body in an aerobics session – you need to exercise as much of your brain as you can in order to keep the whole thing fit and healthy. Just as your body begins to lose its strength and agility as you grow older, so the general effect of ageing on the brain is for it to become less supple and to start to lose its strength, metaphorically speaking. Just consider that there are around 100 billion neurons in your brain – neurons are the brain cells that, among other things, control the main cognitive functions of language, attention, reasoning, memory and visual and spatial awareness. On top of this there are around 100 to 500 *trillion* connections between them, called synapses. Each neuron is linked to between 1,000 and 25,000 others by these synapses, which act like electrical wiring between the active components of a hugely complex computer. Unlike a computer, however, synapses may fade and die if they are not used. A three-year-old child has 1,000 trillion synapses, with at least half having gone by adulthood as a natural part of the brain's tidying-up process that starts at puberty. A good brain workout can help prevent further decline, and build new ways of thinking.

The Importance of Sleep

The general effect of regular brain exercise can potentially extend to improving the memory, to sharpening the mind and to slowing down the whole process of mental decline. Exercise, however, is not the only requirement for a fit and healthy brain. Just as you need a healthy day-to-day life to maintain a healthy body, so the same is true of your brain. Sleep is one of the key factors in keeping your brain in top form, and reducing stress. Having proper rest is every bit as important as taking proper exercise, but sleeping well is not always as easy as we might hope.

Every aspect of your lifestyle is linked in almost as many ways as the neurons in your brain. Many factors can interfere with sleep, but looking after yourself properly is a critically important step. Falling into bed at midnight having spent the entire evening drinking, before tucking into a greasy hamburger on the way home, is not the way to achieve restful sleep – especially if you know you will have to be awake again in a few hours to go to work. Although some people can manage perfectly well with less, most of us need at least seven to eight hours of sleep each night. If you find it difficult to get to sleep, you may need to look at a variety of things that can conspire to keep you awake. Eating late at night or drinks with a high caffeine content, such as tea, coffee and some fizzy drinks, can make it harder to sleep.

Although you might think that drinking alcohol helps you to relax, and may well help you to fall asleep, heavy drinking is not the best way to achieve a good night's rest. The detrimental effects of overdrinking are quite horrific. Even small amounts of alcohol can cause chemical imbalances in the brain that affect our thought patterns and comprehension, as well as impairing our speech, balance and general motor functions. A larger intake of alcohol, consistent with alcohol abuse over an extended period, can make your brain shrink, damage the frontal lobes and cause a whole catalogue of other health problems such as liver damage.

Another potential factor in inhibiting brain power is smoking. The general health hazards involved in smoking are well known, and there is evidence that smoking can actually impair brain function – plus certainly the addictive qualities are not conducive to reducing stress.

A Good Mental Routine

The exercises in *Anti-stress Puzzles* will go some way towards improving your brain fitness, but there are many other forms of mental exercise that you can incorporate into your daily routine. In fact, varying your daily routine will help to keep your mind alert, keep you thinking about what you are doing instead of drifting along 'on automatic pilot' and help keep your brain suitably active. You can start from the moment you get up in the morning simply by brushing your teeth or eating your cereal with the other hand. On the way to a regular destination such as work, why not try getting off the bus a stop or two early and walking the rest of the way, or taking a different route altogether?

INTRODUCTION

Hobbies that make you concentrate in a way that is different from the way you focus on your usual work are also good for activating different areas of the brain. Chess, card games such as bridge, jigsaw puzzles or even knitting all provide a bit of mental exercise as do sports such as tennis or golf, which also improve coordination and general fitness. Maintaining a reasonable level of physical fitness will always help in improving blood circulation and your brain likes nothing better than a healthy flow of blood. Walking, swimming and jogging are all good forms of physical exercise that can be combined with a mental workout such as thinking of a long word, like 'acceleration', and then seeing how many anagrams or other words you can make from it.

Regularly learning new words is a good way to improve your memory. You could even keep a dictionary by your bed, or on your mobile phone, and learn a new word every morning when you get up. Learning a foreign language is another excellent brain-training activity, research having shown that mastering a foreign tongue can provide significant protection against short- and long-term memory loss. It also introduces your brain to new ways of thinking, since each language tends to have words for concepts that are simply not present in other languages.

The Exercises in this Book

All of the puzzles in the book are designed to be fair. They don't require you to guess, and they aren't intended to require an enormous amount of time to solve – although your actual solving times will depend on your familiarity with the puzzle types, so if you are something of a Sudoku expert then you'll probably be faster on the Sudoku puzzles than someone who has never tackled one before. What all of the puzzles do require you to do, however, is to think logically about the problems in front of you. If it's a reasoning puzzle then think about what deductions you can make, or if it's a memory test then think about how you might go about remembering what you need to remember. If it involves any maths and it looks complex then have a think about how you can simplify it. Read the whole question before you start to answer.

Without spoiling any surprises about the types of puzzle and questions you'll encounter in the book, a few general tips could still be useful. The puzzles and tests are designed to make you *think*, so if you're sometimes stuck then that's not necessarily a bad thing! If the question has numbers and units in it, such as miles per hour, then think about what the unit actually is – 'miles per hour' effectively means 'miles divided by hours', so if you're told a train travelled at 40 mph for 15 minutes then that means 'miles divided by hours equals 40', or put another way '40 times hours equals miles'. In a quarter of an hour, therefore, it went 0.25 (hours) times 40 miles, which is equal to 10 miles. A bit of logical thought about the question will often make even the toughest-looking problem much simpler to answer.

If it's a memory test then try building mental pictures in your head. These force you to think and process what you are reading, and if you make them ridiculous then they can be memorable in their own right. For example, if you need to remember 'bicycle' and 'house' then imagine a bicycle flying over a house and you probably won't forget that association. You can build up long chains of imagery such as this and remember a surprisingly large amount of material. Even if you forget it, you'll be making your brain work so you'll still be getting the benefit – and the practice will help improve your memory!

When solving, don't be afraid to make notes of what you've worked out so far. You'll need a pencil to write in some of the answers anyway, so you might as well use it as you go. Of course, if you can keep everything in your head, then so much the better, but if you find yourself glazing over or you find that it's taking too long then just write

INTRODUCTION

things out as you go – it usually helps clarify your thoughts. With some of the logic puzzles, such as Kakuro or Sudoku, making notes in the grid is often key to solving them quickly.

Finally, try to work through at least one of the exercises in this book a few days each week. Even if you spend just a couple of minutes on a puzzle then your brain can still benefit. For example, research has shown that just this small amount of regular brain exercise can make elderly people appear as sharp and alert as people 10 years younger than them. No matter how old you are, your brain is so important to everything you do that you really owe it to yourself to keep it in shape – and hopefully reduce stress as you do so.

Good luck, and have fun!

SUDOKU

Instructions

Sudoku has one very simple rule: place a digit from 1 to 9 in each of the empty squares in the grid, so that each row, column and bold-lined 3×3 box contains every digit exactly once.

9	5	3	2	7	1	6	8	4
6	2	4	3	5	8	7	1	9
8	1	7	4	6	9	3	5	2
4	9	2	7	1	3	8	6	5
1	6	8	5	9	2	4	3	7
3	7	5	6	8	4	9	2	1
5	3	9	8	2	7	1	4	6
7	8	6	1	4	5	2	9	3
2	4	1	9	3	6	5	7	8

Solved example

	9		2			3		7
4				9		5	8	
	7			5			9	2
	2			4		9		1
9	3						5	8
1		8		3		7		
3	4			6		2		
	8	9		7				3
5		7			4	1		

Solving hint: For each number from 1 to 9, check every row, column and 3x3 box to see if there is only one place it can fit in that region. For example, in the top-right 3x3 box there is only one place that a 1 can fit.

6	9	5	2	8	1	3	4	7
4	1	2	7	9	3	5	8	6
8	7	3	4	5	6	1	9	2
7	2	6	5	4	8	9	3	1
9	3	4	6	1	7	2	5	8
1	5	8	9	3	2	6	7	4
3	4	1	8	6	9	7	2	5
2	8	9	1	7	5	4	6	3
5	6	7	3	2	4	8	1	9

Read this tale of tails, and then answer as many questions as you can without checking the text again. Then, when you've done that, go back and check the text again and answer the rest.

Once a week, on Tuesday, Katie goes for a walk in the park with her brother Tom's dog, Sammy. Sammy is a friendly dog and so likes to say hello, in a doggy kind of way, to a mix of canine chums. Particular friends that Sammy always encounters include Woof, the golden retriever owned by the local barber, and Mr Bark, the small spaniel that's frequently found yapping madly at equally small children who dare to attempt a friendly pat. Sammy is a creature of habit, so he will always walk Katie around the park in a clockwise direction, while the other dogs always take their owners around the path in an anti-clockwise direction on Tuesdays. On Wednesdays, when Sammy isn't there, Woof goes the other way.

Occasionally, a neighbourhood cat has the temerity to wander across what is clearly Sammy's park. Katie's tortoiseshell, Black, is just such a cat, although she knows better than to visit when Sammy's around. On other days of the week, she likes to bully the window cleaner's yappy little Jack Russell – the one that isn't quite so brave as his yappy little mouth would like you to think.

This cat and dog life has been going on for the best part of three years now, so maybe it's time for things to change – Sammy's even considering walking the other way around the park. Of course, that might cause a problem with maintaining his territorial rights, so he's not sure; maybe he'll try it next week.

- Which way around the park does Mr Bark walk?
- On what days of the week do we know the barber's dog visits the park?
- What colour is Black?
- What job does the Jack Russell's owner have?
- What is the relationship between Katie and Tom?
- Which dogs do we know sometimes or always walk clockwise around the park?
- How many different people are mentioned by name?
- How many times is the word 'chums' used in this story?
- On what day of the week does the cat in the story normally avoid the park?
- What sort of dog is Woof?
- When is Sammy considering walking the other way around the park?
- How many cats are mentioned by name in this story?

15

Which way around the park does Mr Bark walk?
Anti-clockwise

On what days of the week do we know the barber's dog visits the park?
Tuesday and Wednesday

What colour is Black?
Tortoiseshell

What job does the Jack Russell's owner have?
Window cleaner

What is the relationship between Katie and Tom?
Siblings (Tom is Katie's brother)

Which dogs do we know sometimes or always walk clockwise around the park?
Sammy and Woof

How many different people are mentioned by name?
Two

How many times is the word 'chums' used in this story?
Once

On what day of the week does the cat in the story normally avoid the park?
Tuesday

What sort of dog is Woof?
Golden retriever

When is Sammy considering walking the other way around the park?
Next week

How many cats are mentioned by name in this story?
One

KAKURO

Instructions

Place a digit from 1 to 9 into each white square. Each horizontal run of white squares must add up to the total above the diagonal line to the left of the run, and each vertical run of white squares must add up to the total below the diagonal line above the run. **No digit can be used more than once in any run.**

Solved example

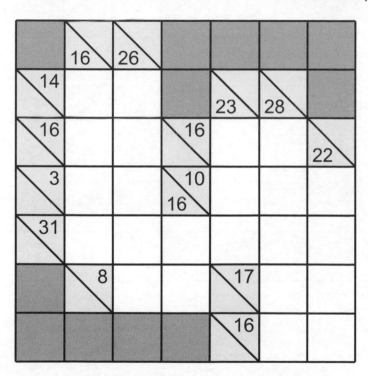

Solving hint: Start by considering the square where the '16' and '23' clues intersect. The solution to the '16' must be 7+9, while the solution to the '23' must be 6+8+9. This means the only number in common is 9, so that value must go in the intersecting square.

If you get stuck, copy a few solution digits back into the grid from the next page in order to get you started.

	16	26				
14	6	8		23	28	
16	7	9	16	9	7	22
3	1	2	10 / 16	6	3	1
31	2	6	9	8	1	5
	8	1	7	17	8	9
				16	9	7

SHAPE COUNT

Look at the drawing below, then answer the questions that refer to it:

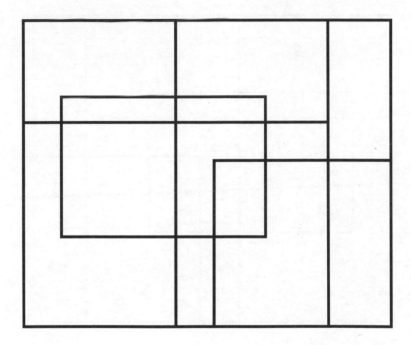

- How many corners (⌐⌐⌐⌐), not counting 'T' or '+' junctions, are there in this illustration?

- How many rectangles can you form by tracing along the lines in various ways?

- How many different colours would you need to colour in the interior of each shape so that no two coloured shapes were touching one another (not counting diagonal touching)?

- How many intersections are there where a '+' sign is formed?

- And how many intersections are there where a 'T' is formed?

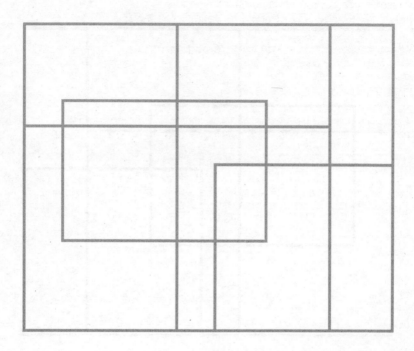

How many corners (⌐⌐⌐⌐), not counting 'T' or '+' junctions, are there in this illustration?
9

How many rectangles can you form by tracing along the lines in various ways?
28

How many different colours would you need to colour in the interior of each shape so that no two coloured shapes were touching one another (not counting diagonal touching)?
3

How many intersections are there where a '+' sign is formed?
8

And how many intersections are there where a 'T' is formed?
8

MIXED PUZZLES

See how quickly you can complete the following puzzles:

Which of these words is the odd one out, and why?

Italy   France   Paris   Spain   Germany

Which number comes next in this sequence?

7   9   12   16   _____

Fire engine is to fire station, as ambulance is to... what?

Which of these numbers would look the same if viewed upside down?

123   765   906   938   578   112   656

How many minutes are there in 5 hours?

If my normal 30-minute journey somehow takes me 45 minutes today, and I normally drive at 45 mph, how fast did I drive today?

If the temperature rises from 6°C to 27°C, by how many degrees Celsius has it risen?

Complete the following:

12 x 3 = _____   96 – 14 = _____   15 x 3 = _____

True or false: a tonne of feathers weighs less than a tonne of steel?

Which letter comes next in this pattern?

A A B A B C A B C D A B C ?

Complete the following:

123 + 15 = _____   27 ÷ 3 = _____   57 – 12 = _____

If I rapidly press the '2' button on my mobile phone I select A, then B, then C. How many times do I need to press '2' to type 'CAB'?

Which of these words are not palindromes? A palindrome is a word or phrase that reads the same both forwards and backwards.

Dad   Mum   Son   Bob   Bro   Sis

If forty-three people go to the park, then another twelve, but then thirty-three leave, how many people remain in the park?

Which of these words is the odd one out, and why?
Paris – the only one that isn't a country

Which number comes next in this sequence?
21 – the difference increases by 1 at each step

Fire engine is to fire station, as ambulance is to... what?
Hospital

Which of these numbers would look the same if viewed upside down?
906

How many minutes are there in 5 hours?
300 minutes

If my normal 30-minute journey somehow takes me 45 minutes today, and I normally drive at 45 mph, how fast did I drive today?
30 mph

If the temperature rises from 6°C to 27°C, by how many degrees Celsius has it risen?
21°C

Complete the following:
$12 \times 3 = \mathbf{36}$ $96 - 14 = \mathbf{82}$ $15 \times 3 = \mathbf{45}$

True or false: a tonne of feathers weighs less than a tonne of steel?
False – they both weigh a tonne

Which letter comes next in this pattern?
D – the pattern is 'A', 'A B', 'A B C', 'A B C D' etc, growing one letter longer at each repetition

Complete the following:
$123 + 15 = \mathbf{138}$ $27 \div 3 = \mathbf{9}$ $57 - 12 = \mathbf{45}$

If I press the '2' button on my mobile phone I select A, then B, then C. How many times do I need to press '2' to type 'CAB'?
6 times

Which of these words are not palindromes? A palindrome is a word or phrase that reads the same both forwards and backwards.
Son and Bro

If forty-three people go to the park, then another twelve, but then thirty-three leave, how many people remain in the park?
Twenty-two

WORDSEARCH

Try to find all of the listed animals that are camouflaged in this wordsearch grid. Words can be written forwards or backwards in any direction, including diagonally.

L	G	O	O	U	E	I	U	L	E	A	L
R	R	A	G	R	E	T	S	M	A	H	H
L	C	H	D	U	S	R	L	L	A	M	A
L	A	N	O	M	I	N	A	L	T	A	S
F	N	I	G	I	O	N	L	U	N	R	S
R	A	B	B	I	T	I	E	T	G	M	G
O	U	E	L	I	R	M	E	A	J	A	T
G	G	I	G	O	O	A	I	C	P	D	J
F	I	E	G	U	T	A	F	E	T	I	N
M	R	G	S	E	N	T	A	F	W	L	G
R	M	E	R	T	U	R	T	L	E	L	M
L	E	W	L	Y	R	Y	E	K	N	O	M

ANTEATER   GORILLA   MONKEY
APE   GUINEA PIG   MOUSE
ARMADILLO   HAMSTER   NEWT
CAT   IGUANA   RABBIT
DOG   JAGUAR   TIGER
FROG   LION   TORTOISE
GIRAFFE   LLAMA   TURTLE

```
L G O O U E I U L E A L
R R A G R E T S M A H H
L C H D U S R L L A M A
L A N O M I N A L T A S
F N I G I O N L U N R S
R A B B I T I E T G M G
O U E L I R M E A J A T
G G I G O O A I C P D J
F I E G U T A F E T I N
M R G S E N T A F W L G
R M E R T U R T L E L M
L E W L Y R Y E K N O M
```

Slitherlink

Draw a single loop by connecting some dots with horizontal and vertical lines so that each numbered square has the specified number of adjacent line segments. The loop cannot cross or touch itself.

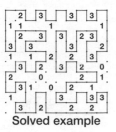

Solved example

3		2		3	
		1	0	2	1
3	2				2
3				2	3
2	2	2	2		
	2		1		3

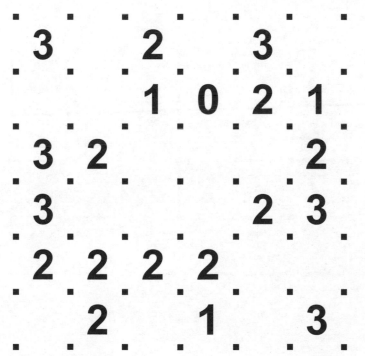

Solving hint: Start by considering the ‘3’ clues. For example, in the top-left corner the loop must run around the top-left of the ‘3’, else it can’t have more than two sides used. Similarly, for the other ‘3’ in the top-row, the loop must run down to the corner of the ‘0’ and then across, since the ‘0’ essentially provides four more ‘corners’.

Then, in the middle of the left-hand column, the loop must run around both ‘3’s consecutively, in either an 5 or 2 pattern.

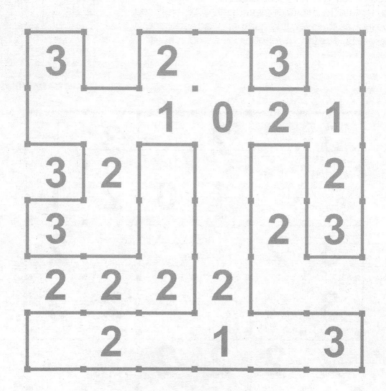

SUDOKU

Instructions

Sudoku has one very simple rule: place a digit from 1 to 9 in each of the empty squares in the grid, so that each row, column and bold-lined 3×3 box contains every digit exactly once.

9	5	3	2	7	1	6	8	4
6	2	4	3	5	8	7	1	9
8	1	7	4	6	9	3	5	2
4	9	2	7	1	3	8	6	5
1	6	8	5	9	2	4	3	7
3	7	5	6	8	4	9	2	1
5	3	9	8	2	7	1	4	6
7	8	6	1	4	5	2	9	3
2	4	1	9	3	6	5	7	8

Solved example

	9	8	6					
7			3			1	2	
1								6
5	6			2	3	9		8
9	8		1		7		4	3
3		4	8	5			1	2
4								1
	2	7			1			5
					8	3	9	

2	9	8	6	1	5	7	3	4
7	5	6	3	8	4	1	2	9
1	4	3	7	9	2	8	5	6
5	6	1	4	2	3	9	7	8
9	8	2	1	6	7	5	4	3
3	7	4	8	5	9	6	1	2
4	3	9	5	7	6	2	8	1
8	2	7	9	3	1	4	6	5
6	1	5	2	4	8	3	9	7

MEMORY

Spend a few minutes memorizing these fruits, including which box each fruit is in.

When you turn the page, you'll be asked to recall the fruit and write them into the corresponding boxes. The initial letters will be given.

Apple	Pear	Banana	Satsuma
Orange	Peach	Cherry	Grape
Lychee	Pineapple	Date	Raspberry
Strawberry	Pomegranate	Elderberry	Watermelon

SOLUTION

Now try to fill in the table without checking back to the previous page. All of
the initial letters are given to help you.

A	P	B	S
O	P	C	G
L	P	D	R
S	P	E	W

KAKURO

Instructions

Place a digit from 1 to 9 into each white square. Each horizontal run of white squares must add up to the total above the diagonal line to the left of the run, and each vertical run of white squares must add up to the total below the diagonal line above the run. **No digit can be used more than once in any run.**

Solved example

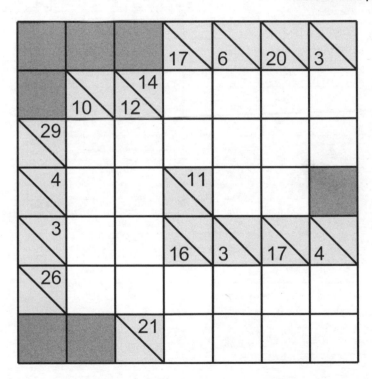

Solving hint: Start by considering the square where the '17' and '14' overlap. The solution to the '17' must be 8+9, but if the 9 was in the intersecting square then this would leave a total of 5 in the three remaining squares in that row, which is impossible (the minimum total of three squares is 1+2+3 = 6). So the value in the intersecting square must be 8.

If you get stuck, copy a few solution digits back into the grid from the next page in order to get you started.

			17\	6\	20\	3\
	10\	12\14	8	1	3	2
\29	2	6	9	3	8	1
\4	3	1	\11	2	9	
\3	1	2	16\	3\	17\	4\
\26	4	3	7	2	9	1
		\21	9	1	8	3

MIXED PUZZLES

Try this page of mixed puzzles:

Which of these words is the odd one out, and why?

Tool   **Heel**   **Baas**   **Tale**   **Keel**

What number comes next in this sequence?

19   15   11   7   _____

Food is to eat, as water is to... what?

Which of these numbers would look the same if viewed in a mirror?

456   656   609   808   919   403   717

If it's 2:45 pm now, what time will it be in two and a half hours?

If Bob drives at 70 mph for 20 minutes, then 30 mph for 5 minutes followed by 70 mph for 10 minutes, how long does his journey take?

How many hours are there in a week?

Complete the following:

5 + 15 + 25 = _____   **9 × 13 = _____**   **171 − 116 = _____**

True or false: if I was born in 1973, and it's 2015 now, then I must be 42 years old?

Which letter comes next in this pattern?

A C D A C D A C ?

Complete the following:

987 + 55 = _____   **545 − 442 = _____**   **13 × 12 = _____**

How many button presses do I need to type the number 5,432,670 into my calculator?

Which of these words is spelled incorrectly?

Plentiful   Doubts   Seperate   Introduce   Conclude

If I buy two packets of chips and give one away, then buy two more but eat one, how many full packets do I now have?

SOLUTION

Which of these words is the odd one out, and why?
Tale – it is the only one without a double letter in the middle

What number comes next in this sequence?
3 – the number gets 4 less at each step

Food is to eat, as water is to... what?
Drink

Which of these numbers would look the same if viewed in a mirror?
808

If it's 2:45 pm now, what time will it be in two and a half hours?
5:15pm

If Bob drives at 70 mph for 20 minutes, then 30 mph for 5 minutes followed by 70 mph for 10 minutes, how long does his journey take?
It takes 35 minutes – the speeds are unimportant

How many hours are there in a week?
168 hours

Complete the following:
$5 + 15 + 25 =$ **45** $\qquad 9 \times 13 =$ **117** $\qquad 171 - 116 =$ **55**

True or false: if I was born in 1973, and it's 2015 now, then I must be 42 years old?
False – I might be 41, depending on the exact dates

Which letter comes next in this pattern?
A C D A C D A C ?
D – the pattern simply repeats in groups of three letters, A C D

Complete the following:
$987 + 55 =$ **1042** $\quad 545 - 442 =$ **103** $\qquad 13 \times 12 =$ **156**

How many button presses do I need to type the number 5,432,670 into my calculator?
7 button presses – the commas aren't typed

Which of these words is spelled incorrectly?
Seperate – it should be 'separate'

If I buy two packets of chips and give one away, then buy two more but eat one, how many full packets do I now have?
Two packets

WORDSEARCH

Try to find all of these music styles within this wordsearch grid. Words can be written forwards or backwards in any direction, including diagonally.

I	C	C	C	C	T	E	I	F	O	L	K
E	U	G	F	U	S	I	O	N	I	O	E
N	N	T	S	U	B	S	H	U	D	Y	O
H	A	I	O	L	P	C	Y	D	R	I	P
P	D	H	U	Y	E	E	T	T	U	J	E
E	I	E	L	T	L	N	N	J	E	I	R
S	S	A	R	G	E	U	L	B	A	J	A
S	C	A	N	I	O	C	S	N	G	Z	A
F	O	U	B	C	K	S	N	D	G	N	Z
O	J	M	U	K	N	U	P	A	E	L	Y
E	A	E	G	R	U	N	G	E	R	E	L
J	P	U	L	R	F	F	K	L	L	T	M

AMBIENT	FUNK	JUNGLE
BLUEGRASS	FUSION	OPERA
BLUES	GOSPEL	PUNK
CALYPSO	GRUNGE	REGGAE
COUNTRY	HOUSE	SOUL
DISCO	INDIE	TECHNO
FOLK	JAZZ	TRANCE

```
I  C  C  C  C  T  E  I  F  O  L  K
E  U  G  F  U  S  I  O  N  I  O  E
N  N  T  S  U  B  S  H  U  D  Y  O
H  A  I  O  L  P  C  Y  D  R  I  P
P  D  H  U  Y  E  E  T  T  U  J  E
E  I  E  L  T  L  N  N  J  E  I  R
S  S  A  R  G  E  U  L  B  A  J  A
S  C  A  N  I  O  C  S  N  G  Z  A
F  O  U  B  C  K  S  N  D  G  N  Z
O  J  M  U  K  N  U  P  A  E  L  Y
E  A  E  G  R  U  N  G  E  R  E  L
J  P  U  L  R  F  F  K  L  L  T  M
```

SUDOKU

Instructions

Sudoku has one very simple rule: place a digit from 1 to 9 in each of the empty squares in the grid, so that each row, column and bold-lined 3×3 box contains every digit exactly once.

9	5	3	2	7	1	6	8	4
6	2	4	3	5	8	7	1	9
8	1	7	4	6	9	3	5	2
4	9	2	7	1	3	8	6	5
1	6	8	5	9	2	4	3	7
3	7	5	6	8	4	9	2	1
5	3	9	8	2	7	1	4	6
7	8	6	1	4	5	2	9	3
2	4	1	9	3	6	5	7	8

Solved example

		1	7		8	3	6	
	6	3	4		2		9	1
	8			6		4		
5		7						
	3	4				6	2	
						5		9
		6		3			5	
3	2		6		7	9	1	
	4	8	5		1	7		

4	5	1	7	9	8	3	6	2
7	6	3	4	5	2	8	9	1
2	8	9	1	6	3	4	7	5
5	9	7	2	8	6	1	4	3
8	3	4	9	1	5	6	2	7
6	1	2	3	7	4	5	8	9
1	7	6	8	3	9	2	5	4
3	2	5	6	4	7	9	1	8
9	4	8	5	2	1	7	3	6

Read this strange diary entry and then answer as many questions as you can without checking the text again. Then, go back and read the text one more time and see if you can answer the remaining questions.

On a cold day, the wind blows from the north-west; on a warm day it often comes from the south. Today it's very cold, but the wind is still from the south.

The wind is a pain. But not as much as the rain. The rain is persistent, and when it's not raining I'm sure it's simply waiting to rain again. It's been persistently raining since last week, or perhaps the week before that – yes, since Tuesday two weeks ago. It hasn't been dry since.

I've never really understood the weather. The weather is like a word I can't quite spell. It's at the edge of my mind; that feeling where if you could only think of the first letter you're sure you'd work it out. But I never do.

I watch the TV weather forecast, but I'd be better guessing myself. What do they know? They only see a computer screen, not the real world. I see it blow in the trees; hail in the stream; gale in the night; die in the morning.

It's always the morning when it goes quiet. It tempts you out of the house, like a sugar cube to lead a horse – but it's a lie. It's isn't going to carry on like that; it just gets you in its path. Then it springs the aqueous trap. It falls in torrents, iced with thunder storms and lightning.

But surely it must be summer soon? This winter is too long. The nights are too dark, and the mornings too short. The wind comes and goes, beating the house; a cocky pugilist, fighting the church bell and taunting the weather vane – which spins and spins and squeaks and squeaks and keeps me up all night. I suppose I should get double-glazing, but I'd still hear the banging of the barn doors. I should fix those too. Ultimately, I just don't like the wind.

- Which way is the wind coming from today?
- What is that squeaks and keeps me awake?
- What day has it been raining since?
- What do I 'suppose I should get' to make it quieter at night?
- At what time of day does the weather usually go quiet?
- What writing task do I liken predicting the weather to?
- How do I suggest leading a horse?
- What makes a banging sound at night?
- Which direction does the wind usually come from on warm days?
- What have I 'never really understood'?
- How many times do I use the word 'wind'?

Which way is the wind coming from today?
The south

What is that squeaks and keeps me awake?
The weather vane

What day has it been raining since?
Tuesday two weeks ago

What do I 'suppose I should get' to make it quieter at night?
Double-glazing

At what time of day does the weather usually go quiet?
The morning

What writing task do I liken predicting the weather to?
Spelling

How do I suggest leading a horse?
With a sugar cube

What makes a banging sound at night?
The barn doors

Which direction does the wind usually come from on warm days?
The south

What have I 'never really understood'?
The weather

How many times do I use the word 'wind'?
Five times

SLITHERLINK

Slitherlink

Draw a single loop by connecting some dots with horizontal and vertical lines so that each numbered square has the specified number of adjacent line segments. The loop cannot cross or touch itself.

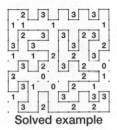

Solved example

2				3
	2		1	1
2	2	2	0		2
2		0	1	1	2
2	3			2	
	2				3

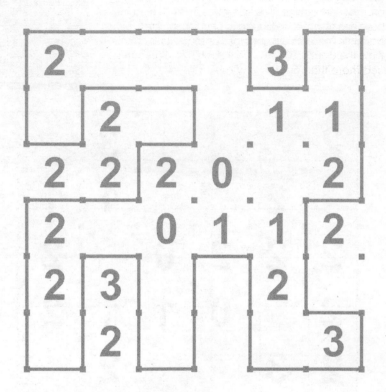

Exercise 16 ◊ Beginner

KAKURO

Instructions

Place a digit from 1 to 9 into each white square. Each horizontal run of white squares must add up to the total above the diagonal line to the left of the run, and each vertical run of white squares must add up to the total below the diagonal line above the run. **No digit can be used more than once in any run.**

Solved example

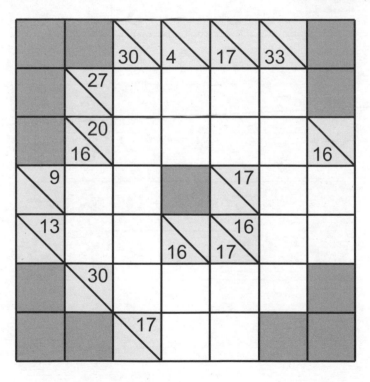

Kakuro solution grid:

		30＼	4＼	17＼	33＼	
	＼27	9	3	8	7	
	＼20 / 16＼	7	1	9	3	16＼
＼9		7	2		＼17	8	9
＼13		9	4	16＼	＼16 / 17	9	7
	＼30	8	7	9	6	
		＼17	9	8		

MIXED PUZZLES

Which of these vehicles is the odd one out, and why?
Train   **Coach**   **Lorry**   **Bus**   **Taxi**

Which number comes next in this sequence?
2   4   8   16 _____

Aeroplane is to pilot as car is to... what?

Answering as quickly as you can, which of these numbers gives the answer 9 if you add up all of its digits?
123   456   135   247   352   128   406

How many hours are there in a weekend, assuming it is not a weekend with a shift to or from daylight saving time?

If I leave the house at 8 am to drive the 10 miles to work at an average of 10 miles per hour, at what time do I arrive?

It was 13°C two days ago. Yesterday the temperature rose 6°C. Today it dropped by 3°C. What is today's temperature?

Complete the following:
20 + 30 − 10 = _____   **99 × 2 =** _____   **30 + 45 =** _____

True or false? If I'm 2 inches taller than Dave, and Dave is 5 inches shorter than Sam, then Sam is 3 inches taller than me.

Which letter comes next in this pattern?
A   B   A   C   A   D   A _____

Complete the following:
300 ÷ 10 = _____   **500 ÷ 5 =** _____   **25 × 30 =** _____

If I turn a combination lock 5 turns right, 3 turns left, 22 turns right and then 4 turns left, how many turns from its starting position does the lock end up?

Which of these words is a palindrome? A palindrome reads the same both forwards and backwards.
Moo   Toot   Food   Tool   Room   Zoo   Pool

If a windmill turns 5 revolutions per hour on a normal day, but twice as many revolutions per hour on a windy day, how may revolutions will it turn in 2 hours on a windy day?

Which of these vehicles is the odd one out, and why?
Lorry – it is the only one that isn't public transport

Which number comes next in this sequence?
2   4   8   16   **32 – the number doubles each time**

Aeroplane is to pilot as car is to **driver**

Answering as quickly as you can, which of these numbers gives the answer 9 if you add up all of its digits?
135 (1+3+5=9)

How many hours are there in a weekend, assuming it is not a weekend with a shift to or from daylight saving time?
48 hours

If I leave the house at 8 am to drive the 10 miles to work at an average of 10 miles per hour, at what time do I arrive?
9 am

It was 13°C two days ago. Yesterday the temperature rose 6°C. Today it dropped by 3°C. What is today's temperature?
16°C

Complete the following:
$20 + 30 - 10 =$ **40** $99 \times 2 =$ **198** $30 + 45 =$ **75**

True or false? If I'm 2 inches taller than Dave, and Dave is 5 inches shorter than Sam, then Sam is 3 inches taller than me.
True

Which letter comes next in this pattern?
A B A C A D A **E – alternating As with B, C, D, E etc**

Complete the following:
$300 \div 10 =$ **30** $500 \div 5 =$ **100** $25 \times 30 =$ **750**

If I turn a combination lock 5 turns right, 3 turns left, 22 turns right and then 4 turns left, how many turns from its starting position does the lock end up?
20 turns (since 5 - 3 + 22 - 4 = 20)

Which of these words is a palindrome? **Toot**

If a windmill turns 5 revolutions per hour on a normal day, but twice as many revolutions per hour on a windy day, how may revolutions will it turn in 2 hours on a windy day?
20 revolutions

MEMORY

Memorize where these vegetables occur in the table. On the next page you'll be asked to recall which vegetable was in which box. Spend a few minutes studying this table, then turn the page once you're ready.

Horseradish	Maris Piper Potato	Cucumber	Asparagus
Endive	Estima Potato	Radish	Carrot
Leek	Parsnip	Spinach	Cauliflower
Pea	Lettuce	Broccoli	Corn on the cob

Now see if you can recall where the vegetables were. Some initial letters are given as clues.

H	M		
E	E		C
L			C
P			C

WORDSEARCH

Can you find all of the listed colours of horse within this wordsearch grid?
Words may be written forwards or backwards in any direction, including
diagonally.

E	L	O	C	S	G	P	I	N	T	O	T
A	T	Y	R	Y	O	N	I	B	L	A	T
P	Y	D	E	P	L	R	I	K	S	F	T
P	A	B	A	R	L	A	R	T	L	S	U
I	B	L	M	R	G	N	E	E	B	K	N
E	D	A	O	O	K	E	A	M	L	E	T
B	O	C	R	M	L	B	S	L	U	W	S
A	O	K	U	G	I	N	A	O	E	B	E
L	L	W	R	T	W	N	U	Y	R	A	H
D	B	E	T	O	T	L	O	D	O	L	C
R	Y	E	R	G	E	L	P	P	A	D	S
N	N	B	C	L	A	Y	B	A	N	K	E

ALBINO
BLACK
BLOOD BAY
BLUE ROAN
BROWN
CHESTNUT
CLAYBANK

CREAM
DAPPLE GREY
DARK BAY
DUN
FLEA-BITTEN
MEALY
PALOMINO

PIEBALD
PINTO
ROSE GREY
SKEWBALD
SORREL
STEEL GREY

49

```
E L O C S G P I N T O T
A T Y R Y O N I B L A T
P Y D E P L R I K S F T
P A B A R L A R T L S U
I B L M R G N E E B K N
E D A O O K E A M L E T
B O C R M L B S L U W S
A O K U G I N A O E B E
L L W R T W N U Y R A H
D B E T O T L O D O L C
R Y E R G E L P P A D S
N N B C L A Y B A N K E
```

SUDOKU

Instructions

Sudoku has one very simple rule: place a digit from
1 to 9 in each of the empty squares in the grid, so that
each row, column and bold-lined 3×3 box contains
every digit exactly once.

9	5	3	2	7	1	6	8	4
6	2	4	3	5	8	7	1	9
8	1	7	4	6	9	3	5	2
4	9	2	7	1	3	8	6	5
1	6	8	5	9	2	4	3	7
3	7	5	6	8	4	9	2	1
5	3	9	8	2	7	1	4	6
7	8	6	1	4	5	2	9	3
2	4	1	9	3	6	5	7	8

Solved example

3	2			5	9		1	7
8	5	7		1	2			
	1		3				8	
5	4					7		
2								9
		6					3	8
	8				4		6	
			5	9		8	7	2
9	3		7	8			4	1

3	2	4	8	5	9	6	1	7
8	5	7	6	1	2	3	9	4
6	1	9	3	4	7	2	8	5
5	4	8	9	3	1	7	2	6
2	7	3	4	6	8	1	5	9
1	9	6	2	7	5	4	3	8
7	8	5	1	2	4	9	6	3
4	6	1	5	9	3	8	7	2
9	3	2	7	8	6	5	4	1

MIXED PUZZLES

Which of these colours is the odd one out, and why?

Green   **Blue**   **Red**   **Orange**   **Black**

Which number comes next in this sequence?

55   66   77   88   99   _____

Intelligent is to unintelligent as open is to?

If I write the number 35,478,353 with its digits in reverse order, which of these do I end up?

35,387,435   35,347,835   35,353,874   35,387,453

Rewrite these times as 24-hour clock times:

1:23 pm   5:30 am   Midnight   8:30 pm   Midday

My friend Simon goes running every day along a 6-mile circuit. It usually takes him an hour to make the circuit, so at what speed does he normally run?

True or false: Tuesday is the day after Monday if you order the days of the week alphabetically?

Complete the following:

99 + 99 = _____   399 – 197 = _____   990 ÷ 99 = _____

How many of these words have fewer consonants than vowels?

Three   Five   Twenty   Seven   Four   Six

Which letter comes next in this pattern?

A B A B C A B C D A _____

Complete the following:

11 + 22 + 33 = _____   541 + 51 = _____   190 + 55 = _____

If I need 2 keys to open my front door, but only 1 to open my back door, how many key turns do I make in total while fully unlocking and then fully locking both doors, assuming both doors were fully locked to start with and all keys require two turns to open or close a lock?

How many of these words have only one vowel?

Monkey   Chimp   Ape   Pie   Trip

If I paint 2 sheds green, 3 sheds blue and 4 sheds yellow, and I use 2 cans of paint per shed, how many cans of paint do I need in total?

Which of these colours is the odd one out, and why?
Black – all the rest are colours of the rainbow

Which number comes next in this sequence?
55   66   77   88   99   **110 – each number increases by 11**

Intelligent is to unintelligent as open is to **closed**

If I write the number 35,478,353 with its digits in reverse order, which of these do I end up?
35,387,453

Rewrite these times as 24-hour clock times:

1:23 pm	5:30 am	Midnight	8:30 pm	Midday
13:23	**05:30**	**00:00**	**20:30**	**12:00**

My friend Simon goes running every day along a 6-mile circuit. It usually takes him an hour to make the circuit, so at what speed does he normally run?
6 miles per hour

True or false: Tuesday is the day after Monday if you order the days of the week alphabetically? **False – the day after Monday would be Saturday**

Complete the following:
99 + 99 = **198**   399 – 197 = **202**   990 ÷ 99 = **10**

How many of these words have fewer consonants than vowels?
None of them!

Which letter comes next in this pattern?
A B A B C A B C D A **B – the sequence is A, AB, ABC, ABCD etc**

Complete the following:
11 + 22 + 33 = **66**   541 + 51 = **592**   190 + 55 = **245**

If I need 2 keys to open my front door but only 1 to open my back door, how many key turns do I make in total while fully unlocking and then fully locking both doors, assuming both doors were fully locked to start with and all keys require two turns to open or close a lock?
12 turns

How many of these words have only one vowel?
Two – chimp and trip

If I paint 2 sheds green, 3 sheds blue and 4 sheds yellow, and I use 2 cans of paint per shed, how many cans of paint do I need in total?
18 cans

Exercise 22 ◊ Beginner

KAKURO

Instructions

Place a digit from 1 to 9 into each white square. Each horizontal run of white squares must add up to the total above the diagonal line to the left of the run, and each vertical run of white squares must add up to the total below the diagonal line above the run. **No digit can be used more than once in any run.**

Solved example

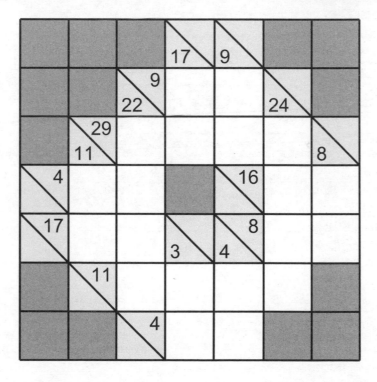

55

			17\	9\		
		22\9	8	1	24\	
	11\29	7	9	8	5	8\
\4	3	1		\16	9	7
\17	8	9	3\	4\8	7	1
	\11	5	2	1	3	
		\4	1	3		

NURIKABE

Instructions

Shade some squares so that each number in the puzzle remains as part of a continuous unshaded area of precisely the given number of squares.

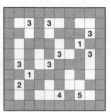

- There must be exactly one number per unshaded area.
- Shaded squares cannot form any 2×2 (or larger) areas
- All shaded squares must form one continuous area. Squares are considered to be continuous if they touch left/right/up/down, but not diagonally.

Solved example

					4
	1				
			3		
		2			
2			1		2

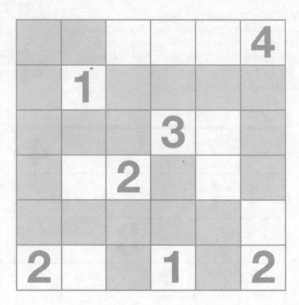

Try to find all of the listed geological eras within this wordsearch grid. Words can be written forwards or backwards in any direction, including diagonally.

N	P	R	E	C	A	M	B	R	I	A	N
S	A	C	N	A	I	R	U	L	I	S	D
I	L	I	E	E	T	E	R	A	U	E	E
L	A	S	C	N	N	N	I	O	N	T	V
J	E	S	O	I	E	E	E	E	R	H	O
U	O	A	T	E	V	C	C	I	C	I	N
R	Z	I	S	A	A	O	O	O	I	T	I
A	O	R	I	T	E	I	D	G	L	U	A
S	I	T	E	A	A	L	C	R	I	O	N
S	C	R	L	O	E	P	D	R	O	L	H
I	C	A	P	P	E	R	M	I	A	N	O
C	P	Q	U	A	T	E	R	N	A	R	Y

CRETACEOUS   ORDOVICIAN   PLIOCENE

DEVONIAN   PALAEOCENE   PRECAMBRIAN

HOLOCENE   PALAEOZOIC   QUATERNARY

JURASSIC   PERMIAN   SILURIAN

OLIGOCENE   PLEISTOCENE   TRIASSIC

```
N P R E C A M B R I A N
S A C N A I R U L I S D
I L I E E T E R A U E E
L A S C N N N I O N T V
J E S O I E E E E R H O
U O A T E V C C I C I N
R Z I S A A O O O I T I
A O R I T E I D G L U A
S I T E A A L C R I O N
S C R L O E P D R O L H
I C A P P E R M I A N O
C P Q U A T E R N A R Y
```

MEMORY

There are 16 types of biscuit in the boxes below. See if you can remember what and where they are so that you put them back in the same boxes on the next page.

Flapjack	Digestive	Pretzel	Shortcake
Cracker	Bourbon	Matzo	Macaroon
Garibaldi	Wafer	Crispbread	Jaffa cake
Ginger nut	Rich tea	Shortbread	Oatcake

Now try to put the biscuits back in the same locations. Four are given for you:

Flapjack			
	Bourbon		
		Crispbread	
			Oatcake

SUDOKU

Instructions

Sudoku has one very simple rule: place a digit from 1 to 9 in each of the empty squares in the grid, so that each row, column and bold-lined 3×3 box contains every digit exactly once.

9	5	3	2	7	1	6	8	4
6	2	4	3	5	8	7	1	9
8	1	7	4	6	9	3	5	2
4	9	2	7	1	3	8	6	5
1	6	8	5	9	2	4	3	7
3	7	5	6	8	4	9	2	1
5	3	9	8	2	7	1	4	6
7	8	6	1	4	5	2	9	3
2	4	1	9	3	6	5	7	8

Solved example

	1		7		2	5	8	
3		7		1		9		6
	5				6			
1					3	7		4
	9	2				3	1	
6		4	1					8
			4				5	
9		3		6		8		7
	6	1	2		8		3	

4	1	6	7	9	2	5	8	3
3	2	7	8	1	5	9	4	6
8	5	9	3	4	6	1	7	2
1	8	5	9	2	3	7	6	4
7	9	2	6	8	4	3	1	5
6	3	4	1	5	7	2	9	8
2	7	8	4	3	9	6	5	1
9	4	3	5	6	1	8	2	7
5	6	1	2	7	8	4	3	9

SLITHERLINK

Slitherlink

Draw a single loop by connecting some dots with horizontal and vertical lines so that each numbered square has the specified number of adjacent line segments. The loop cannot cross or touch itself.

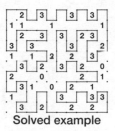

Solved example

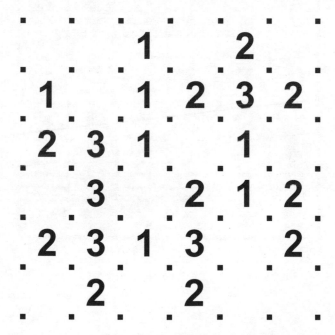

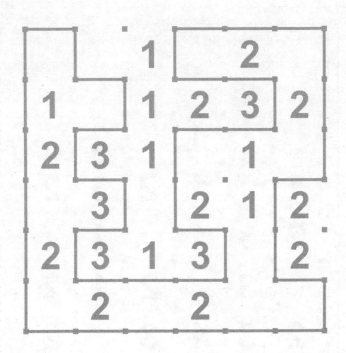

WORDSEARCH

Try to find all of the listed breeds of chicken within this wordsearch grid. Words can be written forwards or backwards in any direction, including diagonally.

P	E	E	N	G	N	I	K	R	O	D	E
P	L	N	L	E	G	H	O	R	N	R	N
R	K	Y	D	S	E	P	P	A	I	E	E
O	H	N	M	G	O	I	I	H	A	L	T
L	O	H	H	O	N	S	S	A	L	C	T
A	U	R	C	G	U	P	R	O	A	E	O
R	D	D	T	L	M	T	R	M	A	T	D
T	A	O	A	A	A	E	H	N	H	N	N
S	N	D	H	M	V	A	O	R	M	A	A
U	N	W	U	A	R	C	Y	W	O	H	Y
A	E	S	F	B	N	I	H	C	O	C	W
N	M	B	E	A	C	R	O	N	I	M	K

ANCONA	DORKING	ORPINGTON
ANDALUSIAN	FAVEROLLE	PLYMOUTH ROCK
AUSTRALORP	HOUDAN	SUMATRA
BRAHMA	LEGHORN	WYANDOTTE
CHANTECLER	MINORCA	
COCHIN	NEW HAMPSHIRE	

```
P E E N G N I K R O D E
P L N L E G H O R N R N
R K Y D S E P P A I E E
O H N M G O I I H A L T
L O H H O N S S A L C T
A U R C G U P R O A E O
R D D T L M T R M A T D
T A O A A A E H N H N N
S N D H M V A O R M A A
U N W U A R C Y W O H Y
A E S F B N I H C O C W
N M B E A C R O N I M K
```

Instructions

Place a digit from 1 to 9 into each white square. Each horizontal run of white squares must add up to the total above the diagonal line to the left of the run, and each vertical run of white squares must add up to the total below the diagonal line above the run. **No digit can be used more than once in any run.**

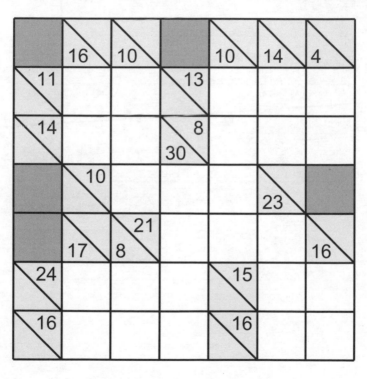

Solved example

69

SOLUTION

	16\	10\		10\	14\	4\
\11	7	4	\13	1	9	3
\14	9	5	30\8	2	5	1
	\10	1	6	3	23\	
	17\	8\21	9	4	8	16\
\24	9	7	8	\15	6	9
\16	8	1	7	\16	9	7

MIXED PUZZLES

Which of these countries is the odd one out, and why?
Argentina   Austria   Brazil   Mexico   Canada

What is the sum of all the numbers from 1 to 9?

Live is to evil as dog is to... what?

How many of these numbers would read the same if viewed upside down?
99   66   696   888

If I'm 140 minutes late for an appointment and arrive at 3:30 pm, what time should I have been there?

I usually leave the house at 8 am for a 20-minute journey into town. Today I made the same journey but left two and a half hours later, and it took three times as long. What time did I arrive in town?

Today it's 70°F, but it's forecast to rise by 11°F during the day and then fall 18°F overnight. What temperature is it forecast to be overnight?

If iron melts at 1538°C, copper melts at 1358K and silicon melts at 2577°F, which melts at the lowest temperature? To convert K to °C, subtract 273.15. To convert °F to °C, subtract 32 and multiply by 5/9.

True or false: if I start off with £200 and give away 25% to charity, I am left with £175.

Which letter comes next in this sequence?
F   S   T   F   F   S   ____

Complete the following:
55 + 555 = ____   505 + 550 = ____   5005 + 505 = ____

If I press the button '4' on my mobile phone I select G, then H, then I. How many times do I need to press '4' to type 'GIG'?

Which of these word pairs are not homophones? (Homophones are words that sound the same but are spelled differently).
Steak & Stake   Mousse & Moose   Mouse & Mice

If a week only had one day in it, how many weeks would there be in a 365-day year?

Which of these countries is the odd one out, and why?
Austria – the only one that isn't in the Americas

What is the sum of all the numbers from 1 to 9? **45**

Live is to evil as dog is to... **God – reverse the letters**

How many of these numbers would read the same if viewed upside down?
One – 888

If I'm 140 minutes late for an appointment and arrive at 3:30 pm, what time should I have been there? **1:10 pm**

I usually leave the house at 8 am for a 20-minute journey into town. Today I made the same journey but left two and a half hours later, and it took three times as long. What time did I arrive in town?
11:30 am

Today it's 70°F, but it's forecast to rise by 11°F during the day and then fall 18°F overnight. What temperature is it forecast to be overnight?
63°F

If iron melts at 1538°C, copper melts at 1358K and silicon melts at 2577°F, which melts at the lowest temperature?
Copper – you don't need to do the full °F to °C conversion, since you can see that half of 2577°F (i.e. less than 5/9ths) is more than 1358K

True or false: if I start off with £200 and give away 25% to charity, I am left with £175.
False – I am donating £50 so I am left with £150

Which letter comes next in this sequence?
F   S   T   F   F   S   **S – the first letters of First, Second, Third, etc**

Complete the following:
55 + 555 = **610**   505 + 550 = **1055**   5005 + 505 = **5510**

If I press the button '4' on my mobile phone I select G, then H, then I. How many times do I need to press '4' to type 'GIG'?
5 times

Which of these word pairs are not homophones? (Homophones are words that sound the same but are spelled differently).
Mouse & Mice

If a week only had one day in it, how many weeks would there be in a 365-day year?
365 weeks

SUDOKU

Instructions

Sudoku has one very simple rule: place a digit from
1 to 9 in each of the empty squares in the grid, so that
each row, column and bold-lined 3×3 box contains
every digit exactly once.

9	5	3	2	7	1	6	8	4
6	2	4	3	5	8	7	1	9
8	1	7	4	6	9	3	5	2
4	9	2	7	1	3	8	6	5
1	6	8	5	9	2	4	3	7
3	7	5	6	8	4	9	2	1
5	3	9	8	2	7	1	4	6
7	8	6	1	4	5	2	9	3
2	4	1	9	3	6	5	7	8

Solved example

9			8	2	7			
1	7							4
	6	2						
7		3	6	4		9		
8				5				2
		6		9	8	1		7
						5	2	
4							9	6
			5	8	6			3

9	5	4	8	2	7	3	6	1
1	7	8	3	6	9	2	5	4
3	6	2	4	1	5	8	7	9
7	2	3	6	4	1	9	8	5
8	1	9	7	5	3	6	4	2
5	4	6	2	9	8	1	3	7
6	3	1	9	7	4	5	2	8
4	8	5	1	3	2	7	9	6
2	9	7	5	8	6	4	1	3

Read this recollection of a musical childhood and then answer as many questions as you can without checking the text again. Then when you've done that go back and check the text and answer the rest.

I had my first tuneless experiments with the piano at the age of six. I only played tunes that used the white keys to start with, and avoided all the black keys, but being six and having grubby hands there was soon little colour difference between the two. I didn't like the notes that played when I pressed the black keys anyway – they were tuneless, like the screeching of my sister's violin.

I did like the trumpet. It was excitingly loud, and my sister didn't approve (although her violin-wailing was hardly quiet). I also tried the flute, but I never could purse my lips correctly. My failed silence was, however, a great success according to my sister.

Drums. They're hard to play out of tune, timpani aside, although you're less likely to play them at all – you don't need many drummers in a school band. It's a shame, since they were even more awesomely noisy than the trumpet, and I had a natural flair for them. Sadly my parents refused to get me a set, so I never really got to learn them. I could have turned out to be a prodigy – who knows? If nothing else, just imagine how much I could have annoyed my sister with them.

I also wanted to learn the guitar, but somehow I never had lessons and I only learnt to play one chord: E major. So I've stuck to the piano. Eventually the black notes became more tuneful, and I started to wash my hands before playing. One day soon they'll call me a latter-day Chopin.

- What instrument couldn't I purse my lips for?
- What phrase do I use to describe the volume of trumpets?
- Which was the only chord I learnt to play on the guitar?
- Which composer's piano playing do I think I'll one day rival?
- What did my sister not approve of?
- How old was I when I first played the piano?
- Which instrument did my sister play?
- What did I have a natural flair for?
- What was a great success, according to my sister?
- Why didn't I like the black notes, originally?
- What two problems stopped me from becoming a drumming prodigy?
- What have I now started to do before playing the piano?

What instrument couldn't I purse my lips for?
Flute

What phrase do I use to describe the volume of trumpets?
Excitingly loud

Which was the only chord I learnt to play on the guitar?
E major

Which composer's piano playing do I think I'll one day rival?
Chopin

What did my sister not approve of?
The trumpet

How old was I when I first played the piano?
Six

Which instrument did my sister play?
Violin

What did I have a natural flair for?
The drums

What was a great success, according to my sister?
My inability to play the flute

Why didn't I like the black notes, originally?
They were tuneless

What two problems stopped me from becoming a drumming prodigy?
Not many drummers were needed in the school band, and my parents wouldn't buy me a set

What have I now started to do before playing the piano?
Wash my hands

KAKURO

Instructions

Place a digit from 1 to 9 into each white square. Each horizontal run of white squares must add up to the total above the diagonal line to the left of the run, and each vertical run of white squares must add up to the total below the diagonal line above the run. **No digit can be used more than once in any run.**

Solved example

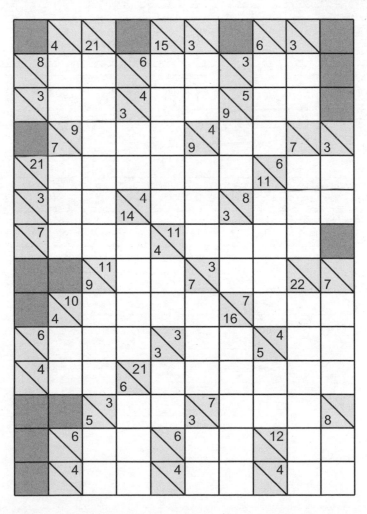

Kakuro solution grid:

Column clues (top row): 4, 21, 15, 3, 6, 3

	4	21		15	3		6	3	
8	3	5	6	4	2	3	2	1	
3	1	2	4 \ 3	3	1	5 \ 9	3	2	
7 \ 9		6	1	2	4 \ 9	3	1	7	3
21	4	3	2	5	1	6	6 \ 11	4	2
3	2	1	4 \ 14	1	3	8 \ 3	5	2	1
7	1	4	2	11 \ 4	5	2	3	1	
		11 \ 9	8	3	3 \ 7	1	2	22	7
	10 \ 4	4	3	1	2	7 \ 16	1	2	4
6	3	2	1	3 \ 3	1	2	4 \ 5	3	1
4	1	3	21 \ 6	1	4	6	3	5	2
		3 \ 5	1	2	7 \ 3	1	2	4	8
	6	4	2	6	2	4	12	7	5
	4	1	3	4	1	3	4	1	3

SHAPE COUNT

Look at the drawing below, then answer the questions that refer to it:

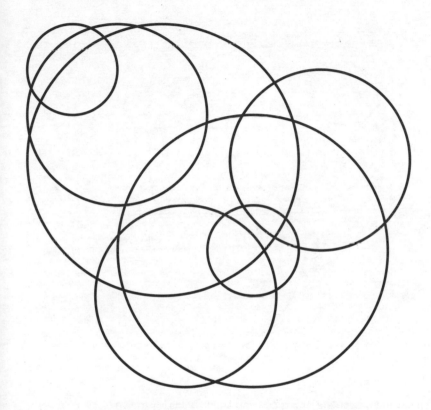

Try to answer these questions without marking on the paper, then mark on the paper and check your answers:

- How many separate circles can you count in this illustration?

- How many intersections are there where the border of one circle crosses the border of another?

- How many separate discrete areas are there in the picture?

- How many different sizes of circle are there?

How many separate circles can you count in this illustration?
7 circles

How many intersections are there where the border of one circle crosses the border of another?
24

How many separate discrete areas are there in the picture?
25

How many different sizes of circle are there?
3

MIXED PUZZLES

Which of these animals is the odd one out, and why?
Monkey   **Squirrel**   **Dog**   **Guinea-pig**   **Cat**

Which number comes next in this sequence?
1   2   3   5   8   _____

If I eat half a cake and then give half of the remainder to my friend, how much of the cake do I have left?

If you write twenty-six million, four hundred thousand and twenty-six out in digits, which of these do you get?
26,400,026   264,026   26,426,000   260,420,026

How many seconds are there in an hour?

If I walk at 3 miles per hour for 50 minutes, how far have I travelled?

Given that water boils at 100°C and iodine boils at 184°C, how many degrees Celsius hotter do I need to heat iodine than water to boil it?

Complete the following:
26 + _____ = 500   45 × _____ = 900   33 + _____ = 660

If there are just three pairs of black and three pairs of white socks in a drawer, how many socks must I take out to be sure of getting one complete pair?

Which letter comes next in this pattern?
Z X Y W X V W ?

Complete the following:
25% of 1000 = _____   15% of 500 = _____   75% of 800 = _____

If a section of fencing has fence posts every 1 metre, and the fence is 5 metres long, how many fence posts are there?

How many of these words have only one consonant?
Ape   Pie   Dog   Kid   Cat   Rib   Due

If I use half a pint of milk to make pancakes on Tuesday, then buy another two pints of milk on Wednesday, of which I use a quarter to make several cups of tea, how much milk do I have left given that I started with two and a half pints?

SOLUTION

Which of these animals is the odd one out, and why?
Guinea-pig – the only one without a visible tail

Which number comes next in this sequence?
13 – add the previous two numbers together

If I eat half a cake and then give half of the remainder to my friend, how much of the cake do I have left?
A quarter

If you write twenty-six million, four hundred thousand and twenty-six out in digits, which of these do you get? **26,400,026**

How many seconds are there in an hour? **3600 seconds**

If I walk at 3 miles per hour for 50 minutes, how far have I travelled?
Two and a half miles

Given that water boils at 100°C and iodine boils at 184°C, how many degrees Celsius hotter do I need to heat iodine than water to boil it?
84°C

Complete the following:
26 + **474** = 500   45 × **20** = 900   33 + **627** = 660

If there are just three pairs of black and three pairs of white socks in a drawer, how many socks must I take out to be sure of getting one complete pair?
4 socks, since the first 3 could all be one colour

Which letter comes next in this pattern?
Z X Y W X V W **U – the sequence Z Y X W is interleaved with the sequence X W V U; each of these is the alphabet in reverse**

Complete the following:
25% of 1000 = **250**   15% of 500 = **75**   75% of 800 = **600**

If a section of fencing has fence posts every 1 metre, and the fence is 5 metres long, how many fence posts are there?
6 – don't forget you need one at the very start and the very end.

How many of these words have only one consonant?
Three – ape, pie and due

If I use half a pint of milk to make pancakes on Tuesday, then buy another two pints of milk on Wednesday, of which I use a quarter of that to make several cups of tea, how much milk do I have left given that I started with two and a half pints?
Three and a half pints

WORDSEARCH

Try to find all of the listed European languages within this wordsearch grid. Words can be written forwards or backwards in any direction, including diagonally.

```
E  A  N  U  C  O  L  N  N  H  C  N  E  R  F  D
N  D  U  T  C  H  N  A  I  S  S  U  R  S  M  G
U  D  U  U  L  R  N  L  P  I  D  I  C  N  H  E
E  R  K  R  L  I  E  A  B  L  E  O  N  N  N  H
H  W  R  K  G  N  N  T  N  G  R  E  E  A  S  A
E  N  A  I  C  I  L  A  G  N  S  U  I  I  D  A
S  O  I  S  S  F  I  C  I  E  E  G  N  N  P  S
W  T  N  H  F  R  T  S  U  N  E  N  N  O  O  L
E  E  I  S  A  N  H  G  I  W  I  E  H  T  L  O
D  R  A  G  L  I  U  U  R  F  I  D  N  S  I  V
I  B  N  A  I  T  A  O  R  C  O  B  R  E  S  E
S  U  A  H  R  A  N  A  I  N  A  B  L  A  H  N
H  C  O  O  I  L  I  O  F  A  E  R  O  E  S  E
E  E  P  H  I  I  A  B  A  S  Q  U  E  E  C  R
S  I  C  E  L  A  N  D  I  C  G  E  R  M  A  N
H  S  L  E  W  N  A  I  S  I  R  F  N  A  G  C
```

ALBANIAN	FINNISH	PORTUGUESE
BASQUE	FRENCH	RUSSIAN
BRETON	FRISIAN	SARDINIAN
CATALAN	GALICIAN	SERBO-CROATIAN
CORNISH	GERMAN	SLOVENE
DANISH	HUNGARIAN	SPANISH
DUTCH	ICELANDIC	SWEDISH
ENGLISH	ITALIAN	TURKISH
ERSE	LITHUANIAN	UKRAINIAN
ESTONIAN	NORWEGIAN	WELSH
FAEROESE	POLISH	

```
E A N U C O L N N H C N E R F D
N D U T C H N A I S S U R S M G
U D U U L R N L P I D I C N H E
E R K R L I E A B L E O N N N H
H W R K G N N T N G R E E A S A
E N A I C I L A G N S U I I D A
S O I S S F I C I E E G N N P S
W T N H F R T S U N E N N O O L
E E I S A N H G I W I E H T L O
D R A G L I U U R F I D N S I V
I B N A I T A O R C O B R E S E
S U A H R A N A I N A B L A H N
H C O O I L I O F A E R O E S E
E E P H I I A B A S Q U E E C R
S I C E L A N D I C G E R M A N
H S L E W N A I S I R F N A G C
```

SLITHERLINK

Slitherlink

Draw a single loop by connecting some dots with horizontal and vertical lines so that each numbered square has the specified number of adjacent line segments. The loop cannot cross or touch itself.

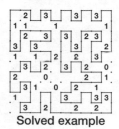

Solved example

```
.   .   .   .   .   .   .   .   .   .
    1   2   1       1
.   .   .   .   .   .   .   .   .   .
  3           0       1   3
.   .   .   .   .   .   .   .   .   .
  2   1       1   0       3
.   .   .   .   .   .   .   .   .   .
        2   1   1       1
.   .   .   .   .   .   .   .   .   .
    1       2   3   1
.   .   .   .   .   .   .   .   .   .
  3     2   2           1   1
.   .   .   .   .   .   .   .   .   .
  3   1   3               2
.   .   .   .   .   .   .   .   .   .
        2       3   2   3
.   .   .   .   .   .   .   .   .   .
```

85

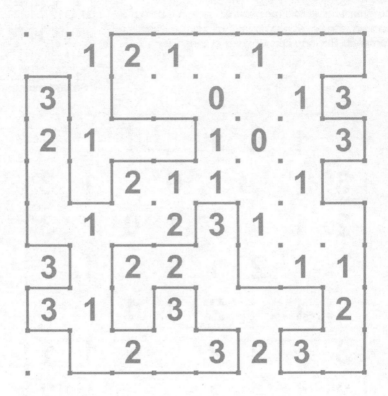

SUDOKU

Instructions

Sudoku has one very simple rule: place a digit from
1 to 9 in each of the empty squares in the grid, so that
each row, column and bold-lined 3×3 box contains
every digit exactly once.

9	5	3	2	7	1	6	8	4
6	2	4	3	5	8	7	1	9
8	1	7	4	6	9	3	5	2
4	9	2	7	1	3	8	6	5
1	6	8	5	9	2	4	3	7
3	7	5	6	8	4	9	2	1
5	3	9	8	2	7	1	4	6
7	8	6	1	4	5	2	9	3
2	4	1	9	3	6	5	7	8

Solved example

				7	1	3		
	7	3		4	6			
9			2				5	
3			8				1	
	1	5				7	9	
	2				5			3
	8				9			4
			1	6		9	2	
		4	7	8				

4	5	8	9	7	1	3	6	2
2	7	3	5	4	6	1	8	9
9	6	1	2	3	8	4	5	7
3	4	6	8	9	7	2	1	5
8	1	5	4	2	3	7	9	6
7	2	9	6	1	5	8	4	3
1	8	2	3	5	9	6	7	4
5	3	7	1	6	4	9	2	8
6	9	4	7	8	2	5	3	1

MEMORY

This grid has 25 rivers listed in it. See if you can remember which box they're in. You *don't* need to remember the names of the rivers themselves – just where they are. Take a few minutes to try to memorize them, then turn the page and place each of the rivers in the given list into the appropriate box.

Severn	Amazon	Nile	Dordogne	Niger
Isis	Jordan	Limpopo	Little Bighorn	Yukon
Volta	Thames	Tweed	Yangtze	Tay
Indus	Rio Grande	Moselle	Tyne	Churchill
Congo	Orinoco	Ouse	Cam	Barrow

Where did the rivers go?

Beware – there are two red herrings which weren't in the original grid!

Moselle	Rio Grande
Barrow	Orinoco
Tay	Thames
Isis	Rhone
Severn	Volta
Little Bighorn	Dordogne
Tweed	Niger
Ouse	Tyne
Nile	Jordan
Clyde	Amazon
Yukon	Indus
Cam	Congo
Churchill	Yangtze
Limpopo	

KAKURO

Instructions

Place a digit from 1 to 9 into each white square. Each horizontal run of white squares must add up to the total above the diagonal line to the left of the run, and each vertical run of white squares must add up to the total below the diagonal line above the run. **No digit can be used more than once in any run.**

Solved example

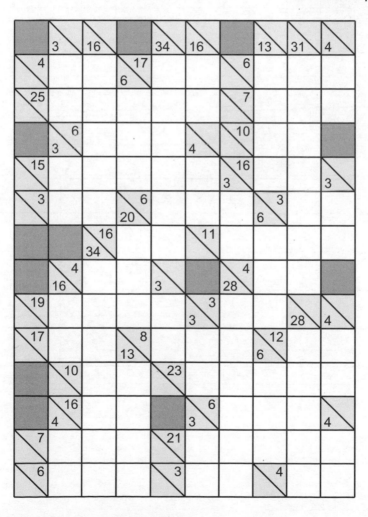

	3\	16\		34\	16\		13\	31\	4\
\4	**1**	**3**	6\17	**8**	**9**	\6	**1**	**2**	**3**
25\	**2**	**6**	**1**	**9**	**7**	\7	**2**	**4**	**1**
3\6		**1**	**2**	**3**	4\	\10	**3**	**7**	
15\	**2**	**4**	**3**	**5**	**1**	3\16	**7**	**9**	3\
3\	**1**	**2**	20\6	**2**	**3**	**1**	6\3	**1**	**2**
	34\16	**9**	**7**	\11	**2**	**3**	**5**	**1**	
16\4	**1**	**3**	3\		28\4	**1**	**3**		
19\	**7**	**3**	**8**	**1**	3\3	**1**	**2**	28\	4\
17\	**9**	**8**	13\8	**2**	**1**	**5**	6\12	**9**	**3**
10\		**7**	**3**	23\	**2**	**9**	**3**	**8**	**1**
4\16		**9**	**7**		3\6	**3**	**2**	**1**	4\
7\	**1**	**4**	**2**	21\	**2**	**8**	**1**	**7**	**3**
6\	**3**	**2**	**1**	3\	**1**	**2**	4\	**3**	**1**

MIXED PUZZLES

Which of these words is the odd one out, and why?
Echo   Lima   Bravo   Gin   Whiskey

Which number comes next in this sequence?
2   3   5   7   11   13   _____

If 50% of statistics are lies, but only 25% of lies are made by statisticians, how many lies are there in the average set of 100 statistics?

Think of a number. Add 15. Multiply by 2. Subtract 24. Subtract 2 times the number you thought of to start with. What number are you left with?

If I get up at 7:30 am and spend an hour getting ready and travelling, then four hours working followed by an hour at lunch, what time will it be when I finish lunch?

If I drive at 60 mph and arrive home at 7 pm, but leave work at 6:15 pm, how many miles is my journey home?

To convert from Celsius to Kelvin you add 273.15. If carbon boils at 3825°C, aluminium boils at 2792°K and nickel boils at 3186°K, which boils at the highest temperature?

Complete the following:
33 + 660 = _____   99 × _____ = 1980   55 × 3 = _____

True or false? If all you know is that on Mondays I always go to the park after work, and on Tuesdays I always go to the zoo at lunchtime, this means that whenever I go to the park it must always be Monday.

Which letter comes next in this pattern?
B C D G J O

Complete the following:
99% of 200 = _____   25% of 600 = _____   55% of 300 = _____

If the Sea of Tranquillity is on the Moon, and the Black Sea is on Earth, on which planet is the Red Sea?

If three-quarters of all supermarkets sell my favourite marmalade, and two-thirds of these don't have it in stock at the moment, what percentage of all supermarkets have my marmalade in stock?

SOLUTION

Exercise 41 ◊ Advanced

Which of these words is the odd one out, and why?
Gin – the only one that isn't a NATO phonetic alphabet letter

Which number comes next in this sequence?
17 – prime numbers in increasing order

If 50% of statistics are lies, but only 25% of lies are made by statisticians, how many lies are there in the average set of 100 statistics?
50 lies; the fact that 25% of lies are made by statisticians is irrelevant

Think of a number. Add 15. Multiply by 2. Subtract 24. Subtract 2 times the number you thought of to start with. What number are you left with?
6 – this will be the result no matter which number you began with

If I get up at 7:30 am and spend an hour getting ready and travelling, then four hours working followed by an hour at lunch, what time will it be when I finish lunch? **1:30 pm**

If I drive at 60 mph and arrive home at 7 pm, but leave work at 6:15 pm, how many miles is my journey home? **45 miles**

To convert from Celsius to Kelvin you add 273.15. If carbon boils at 3825°C, aluminium boils at 2792°K and nickel boils at 3186°K, which boils at the highest temperature? **Carbon, at 4098.15°K**

Complete the following:
33 + 660 = **693**   99 × **20** = 1980   55 × 3 = **165**

True or false? If all you know is that on Mondays I always go to the park after work, and on Tuesdays I always go to the zoo at lunchtime, this means that whenever I go to the park it must always be Monday. **False**

Which letter comes next in this pattern?
B C D G J O **P – curved capital letters in alphabetical order**
Alternative answer: **T, since the letters are 1, 1, 3, 3, 5, 5, etc apart**

Complete the following:
99% of 200 = **198**   25% of 600 = **150**   55% of 300 = **165**

If the Sea of Tranquillity is on the Moon, and the Black Sea is on Earth, on which planet is the Red Sea?
Also Earth – the question is intended to trick you into answering 'Mars'

If three-quarters of all supermarkets sell my favourite marmalade, and two-thirds of these don't have it in stock at the moment, what percentage of all supermarkets have my marmalade in stock?
25%

Try to find all of the listed legumes and pulses within this wordsearch grid. Words can be written forwards or backwards in any direction, including diagonally.

```
A  L  P  A  B  P  B  L  A  C  K  B  E  A  N  T
L  L  I  T  N  E  L  Y  U  P  U  B  L  N  L  S
F  T  A  U  P  E  A  N  U  T  L  A  A  M  I  E
A  N  B  O  R  L  O  T  T  I  B  E  A  N  T  G
L  N  I  R  E  D  I  E  T  L  B  Y  T  A  N  E
F  A  T  P  R  P  R  N  A  D  R  P  A  E  E  R
A  E  B  S  U  B  E  B  E  E  O  E  H  B  L  M
T  B  E  N  E  L  E  Y  D  N  W  T  A  D  N  A
U  D  C  A  N  N  E  L  L  I  N  I  B  E  A  N
O  A  N  E  A  K  E  S  N  I  L  T  C  G  I  L
T  O  E  B  C  N  O  V  C  U  E  S  O  N  T  E
E  R  B  A  T  Y  E  A  C  B  N  P  W  I  P  N
G  B  L  I  B  L  Y  R  L  I  T  O  P  W  Y  T
N  B  L  E  V  H  E  E  E  E  I  I  E  Y  G  I
A  Y  A  E  P  T  I  L  P  S  L  S  A  L  E  L
M  N  T  L  S  O  P  C  A  R  O  B  B  E  A  N
```

ALFALFA	COWPEA	PETITS POIS
BEAN SPROUT	DAL	PUY LENTIL
BLACK BEAN	EGYPTIAN LENTIL	RED LENTIL
BLACK-EYED BEAN	GERMAN LENTIL	SOYBEAN
BORLOTTI BEAN	GREEN LENTIL	SPLIT PEA
BROAD BEAN	HYACINTH	STERCULIA
BROWN LENTIL	LABLAB	URD
BUTTER BEAN	LUPIN	VELVET
CANNELLINI BEAN	MANGETOUT	WINGED BEAN
CAROB BEAN	PEANUT	YAM

SUDOKU

Instructions

Sudoku has one very simple rule: place a digit from 1 to 9 in each of the empty squares in the grid, so that each row, column and bold-lined 3×3 box contains every digit exactly once.

9	5	3	2	7	1	6	8	4
6	2	4	3	5	8	7	1	9
8	1	7	4	6	9	3	5	2
4	9	2	7	1	3	8	6	5
1	6	8	5	9	2	4	3	7
3	7	5	6	8	4	9	2	1
5	3	9	8	2	7	1	4	6
7	8	6	1	4	5	2	9	3
2	4	1	9	3	6	5	7	8

Solved example

				9	3	2		
		2	5		7	9	6	
						7	3	8
			2			3	5	
			1		9			
	6	3			5			
1	4	7						
	3	5	8		2	4		
		6	3	7				

7	8	4	6	9	3	2	1	5
3	1	2	5	8	7	9	6	4
6	5	9	4	2	1	7	3	8
4	9	1	2	6	8	3	5	7
5	7	8	1	3	9	6	4	2
2	6	3	7	4	5	1	8	9
1	4	7	9	5	6	8	2	3
9	3	5	8	1	2	4	7	6
8	2	6	3	7	4	5	9	1

How good are you at remembering what you intended to buy in the grocery store? Read the following story and then answer as many questions as you can without checking the text again. Then, once you've done that, go back and check the text again and answer the rest.

Doug promised he'd do Sally's shopping this weekend. She knew it was a risk, but she was careful to describe the tube of teeth-whitening toothpaste he needed to buy. And the two bags of oranges – the ones on 'buy one get one free'. Oh, and not forgetting a bag of apples (but pick them by hand – don't get the packaged ones). Broccoli too, but make sure it's loose – the pre-wrapped florets are four times as expensive. It's crazy.

Not to mention the bread. Not very exciting, but last time he got the wrong one. He got the thick-sliced, not the thin, and the white, not the wholemeal. And no French loaf at all – apparently a ciabatta looked just as good. But it's not, is it? One's long and pointy; the other one, well, just isn't. I like the point.

Three milks, each four pints, and two orange juices and an apple juice; one-litre cartons for those. Plus don't forget the newspaper on the way in – they didn't have any left at the corner shop this morning – and if the coffee is still on the fifty per cent off offer then make sure you get two or three of those. And teabags. Can't go without tea. Make sure they have the strings to stop them dripping. Get two or three packs of eighty to last the month.

That should do. Oh – and some shampoo (not the green one with the weird texture), some moisturizer (must be marked 'natural') and the spray deodorant with the 'H' logo in the blue bottle. Not the purple one. And then that's it! Well, except for the two C batteries and a pack of forty-watt light bulbs.

Now how could anyone forget any of that?!

- What sort of broccoli shouldn't Doug buy, and why?
- What were Doug's mistakes the last time he bought bread?
- How many litres of juice in total does he have to buy?
- If he forgets just one of the milks, how many pints would he buy?
- What did Doug find just as good as a French loaf?
- What letter identifies the deodorant Sally wants?
- And which other three toiletries does Sally ask Doug to buy?
- What sort of light bulbs does Sally need?
- What's so good about the oranges at the moment?
- What sort of teabag does Sally want?
- What does Doug need to remember on his way into the shop?
- What colour of shampoo will Sally refuse to accept?
- How many batteries does Sally need?

What sort of broccoli shouldn't Doug buy, and why?
Pre-wrapped florets – they cost four times as much

What were Doug's mistakes the last time he bought bread?
He got thick-sliced not thin-sliced, and white not wholemeal

How many litres of juice in total does he have to buy?
Three

If he forgets just one of the milks, how many pints would he buy?
Eight pints

What did Doug find just as good as a French loaf?
A ciabatta

What letter identifies the deodorant Sally wants?
H

And which other three toiletries does Sally ask Doug to buy?
Teeth-whitening toothpaste, natural moisturizer and some shampoo

What sort of light bulbs does Sally need?
Forty-watt

What's so good about the oranges at the moment?
They're on 'buy one get one free'

What sort of teabag does Sally want?
Teabags with anti-drip strings to pull

What does Doug need to remember on his way into the shop?
A newspaper

What colour of shampoo will Sally refuse to accept?
Green

How many batteries does Sally need?
Two

SLITHERLINK

Slitherlink

Draw a single loop by connecting some dots with horizontal and vertical lines so that each numbered square has the specified number of adjacent line segments. The loop cannot cross or touch itself.

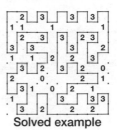

Solved example

```
2  2  3     3  2
      2     2     1  2
2  3  2        2     3
   2     2  1  0  1  2
3  3  2  3  2     3
2     2        2  2  2
3  3     2     2
      1  2     3  2  3
```

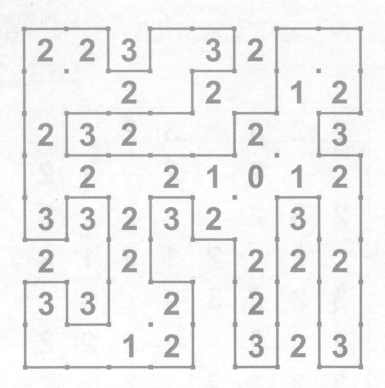

KAKURO

Instructions

Place a digit from 1 to 9 into each white square. Each horizontal run of white squares must add up to the total above the diagonal line to the left of the run, and each vertical run of white squares must add up to the total below the diagonal line above the run. **No digit can be used more than once in any run.**

Solved example

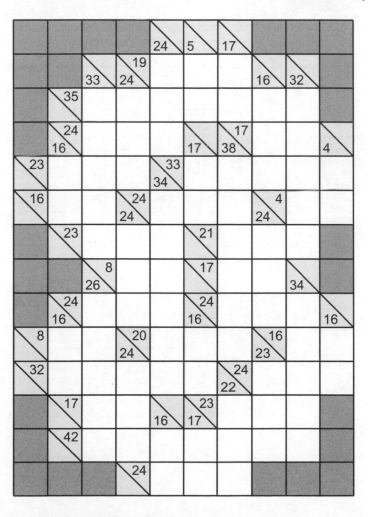

Kakuro solution grid:

				24\	5\	\17			
		\33	19\24	**7**	**3**	**9**	16\	\32	
	\35	**3**	**7**	**9**	**2**	**8**	**1**	**5**	
	24\16	**7**	**9**	**8**	\17	17\38	**8**	**9**	\4
23\	**9**	**6**	**8**	33\34	**9**	**6**	**7**	**8**	**3**
16\	**7**	**9**	24\24	**9**	**8**	**7**	\4 24\	**3**	**1**
	\23	**8**	**9**	**6**	\21	**5**	**9**	**7**	
		8\26	**7**	**1**	\17	**9**	**8**	\34	
	24\16	**9**	**8**	**7**	24\16	**8**	**7**	**9**	\16
8\	**7**	**1**	20\24	**8**	**9**	**3**	16\23	**7**	**9**
32\	**9**	**5**	**8**	**3**	**7**	24\22	**9**	**8**	**7**
	\17	**8**	**9**	16\	23\17	**9**	**8**	**6**	
	\42	**3**	**7**	**9**	**8**	**5**	**6**	**4**	
			\24	**7**	**9**	**8**			

MIXED PUZZLES

Which of these flowers is the odd one out, and why?
Daffodil   **Crocus**   **Iris**   **Daisy**   **Gladiolus**

Which number comes next in this sequence?
12   14   13   15   14   _____

If I roll a die, I have a 1 in 6 chance of getting the number 1. If I roll two dice what is the chance that I get a total of 2?

If politicians only tell the truth on Fridays, but they don't work Fridays in Parliament, how much truth is spoken in Parliament?

If I went to bed at 11:15 pm and got up at 7:30 am, how long was I in bed, assuming the clocks didn't go back or forwards overnight?

I normally drive at an average of 30 mph, but today I need to slow to half my speed due to traffic. If my journey usually takes 20 minutes, how long does it take today?

To convert from Celsius to Fahrenheit you multiply by 9 and then divide by 5, then add 32. If the temperature is 25°C then what is it in Fahrenheit?

True or false: the word 'true' comes after 'false' in the dictionary if you read it backwards, from the last page to the first page?

Which letter comes next in this sequence?
X   L   C   D   _____

Sort these into increasing order of value:
25% of £2   **Half of £3**   **10 ten-pence pieces**

If humans are descended from apes and apes are descended from amoebas, are humans descended from amoebas?

Which of these word pairs are not synonyms? (Synonyms are words which can have the same meaning)
Rich & Wealthy   Happy & Sad   Far & Distant   Clear & Obvious

If a section of fencing has fence posts every 2 metres, and the fence is 56 metres long, how many fence posts are there?

SOLUTION Exercise 47 ◊ Advanced

Which of these flowers is the odd one out, and why?
Daisy – the only flower that doesn't grow from a bulb

Which number comes next in this sequence?
16 – the pattern is add 2, subtract 1, add 2, subtract 1, etc

If I roll a die, I have a 1 in 6 chance of getting the number 1. If I roll two dice what is the chance that I get a total of 2?
1 in 36 – you multiply 1-in-6 by 1-in-6 to get 1-in-36

If politicians only tell the truth on Fridays, but they don't work Fridays in Parliament, how much truth is spoken in Parliament?
None

If I went to bed at 11:15 pm and got up at 7:30 am, how long was I in bed, assuming the clocks didn't go back or forwards overnight?
8 hours 15 minutes

I normally drive at an average of 30 mph, but today I need to slow to half my speed due to traffic. If my journey usually takes 20 minutes, how long does it take today?
40 minutes – you don't need to know I normally drive at 30 mph

To convert from Celsius to Fahrenheit you multiply by 9 and then divide by 5, then add 32. If the temperature is 25°C then what is it in Fahrenheit?
77°F

True or false: the word 'true' comes after 'false' in the dictionary if you read it backwards, from the last page to the first page? **False**

Which letter comes next in this sequence?
X   L   C   D   **M – Roman numerals in increasing value**

Sort these into increasing order of value:
25% of £2 (50p), 10 ten-pence pieces (£1), Half of £3 (£1.50)

If humans are descended from apes and apes are descended from amoebas, are humans descended from amoebas?
Yes

Which of these word pairs are not synonyms? (Synonyms are words which can have the same meaning)
Happy & Sad

If a section of fencing has fence posts every 2 metres, and the fence is 56 metres long, how many fence posts are there?
29, including the ones at both ends

MEMORY

Here are 25 words arranged in a grid. This time you will need to remember not only the words but also which box they're in. These are all common English words so, with the right memory techniques, they may be easier to remember than the specialist lists in earlier memory tasks.

Spend a few minutes trying to learn the following:

Dog	Leg	Monday	Park	Roundabout
Doll	Puddle	Weather	Night	Tuesday
Door	Television	Trampoline	Child	Zoo
Wednesday	Library	Shopping	Trainers	Party
Drink	Key	Car	Bed	Thursday

Try to recall the words that were in the grid, and their positions:

Dog				

If you had difficulty with this then you might find it easier to remember the words and their order if you try memorizing them as a story – for example, 'the **dog** bit my **leg** on **Monday**; I was in the **park** on the **roundabout**; a **doll** was in a **puddle** caused by the bad **weather**', and so on. Feel free to have a second go at this task!

WORDSEARCH

Try to find all of the listed sports within this wordsearch grid. Words can be written forwards or backwards in any direction, including diagonally.

```
F Y K L O J Y N K C R O Q U E T
I L A B D N A H E O G N I W O R
K C O O L O P V D I S C U S U U
G Y E G G T E S E L G N A G F N
E C A B N N A G K L L A B T E N
T L E B I I N N S A I Y A S N I
E I A V E M F I O C T N C L C N
K N N O O D I R B R G I E N I G
C G G L N A I E U O T G N S N L
I N L L A B T E K S A B N G G I
R S I E C I T T A S D O L N N D
C K N Y O A I N S E O N I I I I
I I G B R H M E S K N T I L L N
D I O A N Y R I E I I T N W R G
N N K L G D A R C H E R Y O U N
C G L L A B T O O F D Y R B C D
```

ANGLING	DRESSAGE	ORIENTEERING
ARCHERY	FENCING	POLO
BADMINTON	FOOTBALL	ROWING
BASKETBALL	GLIDING	RUGBY
BOWLING	GOLF	RUNNING
CANOEING	GYMNASTICS	SKATING
CRICKET	HANDBALL	SKIING
CROQUET	JAVELIN	SNOOKER
CURLING	KARATE	VOLLEYBALL
CYCLING	LACROSSE	WINDSURFING
DISCUS	NETBALL	

```
F Y K L O J Y N K C R O Q U E T
L L A B D N A H E O G N I W O R
K C O O L O P V D I S C U S U U
G Y E G G T E S E L G N A G F N
E C A B N N A G K L L A B T E N
T L E B I I N N S A I Y A S N I
E I A V E M F I O C T N C L C N
K N N O O D I R B R G I E N I G
C G G L N A I E U O T G N S N L
I N L L A B T E K S A B N G G I
R S I E C I T T A S D O L N N D
C K N Y O A I N S E O N I I I I
I I G B R H M E S K N T I L L N
D I O A N Y R I E I I T N W R G
N N K L G D A R C H E R Y O U N
C G L L A B T O O F D Y R B C D
```

SUDOKU-X

Instructions

Place a digit from 1 to 9 in each of the empty squares in the grid, so that each row, column, bold-lined 3×3 box **and marked diagonal** contains every digit exactly once.

5	9	6	8	1	3	7	2	4
4	1	2	6	9	7	5	3	8
3	7	8	2	5	4	6	9	1
7	5	3	4	8	1	9	6	2
1	6	9	3	2	5	8	4	7
8	2	4	7	6	9	1	5	3
6	4	5	1	7	2	3	8	9
2	8	1	9	3	6	4	7	5
9	3	7	5	4	8	2	1	6

Solved example

							9	
5	1	2	9					
					6		2	
				7			5	3
			6		2			
9	4		1					
	7		2					
					8	6	4	9
	3							

111

6	8	4	7	2	3	1	9	5
5	1	2	9	8	4	7	3	6
3	9	7	5	1	6	4	2	8
2	6	1	8	4	7	9	5	3
7	5	3	6	9	2	8	1	4
9	4	8	1	3	5	2	6	7
4	7	6	2	5	9	3	8	1
1	2	5	3	7	8	6	4	9
8	3	9	4	6	1	5	7	2

MIXED PUZZLES

Which of these letters is the odd one out, and why?

C   O   H   X   N

Which number comes next in this sequence?

4   9   15   22   _____

If I throw three coins up in the air, what is the likelihood that they all land showing heads?

If I can type a five-letter name in 5 seconds and it takes me 6 seconds to type a six-letter name, but I can never find the W key and so it takes me three times as long to type 'W'/'w' than any other letter, which name can I type faster – Wally or Andrew?

It takes me 15 minutes to cycle to work at 10 miles per hour. If I cycle to and from work each day, how many miles in total is my daily cycle ride?

If Dave's sister marries Bob's brother, what relation is Bob to Dave?

Complete the following:

99 × 9 = _____   123 × 3 = _____   72 + 71 = _____

If Pete and Jane have 5 children, and each of their 5 children have 4 more children, and then half of those 4 children have 3 children of their own but the other half only have 2 children, how many great-grandchildren do Pete and Jane have?

Which letter comes next in this sequence:

A   B   b   c   C   D   d   e   _____

If I weigh 80kg and pick up a kilogram of heavy potatoes, while my friend weights 81kg but picks up a kilogram of only light flowers, who now weighs the most in total?

If Tuesdays were only half the length of a normal day, how many complete weeks would there be in a year that started on a Monday given that the year would otherwise have 365 days that are each 24 hours long?

How many upper-case letters look the same when reflected in a mirror?

If bread and milk currently cost a total of £1, of which the bread accounts for 40p, how much will the milk cost if the price goes up by 10%?

Which of these letters is the odd one out, and why?
X – the only letter that isn't a chemical element symbol

Which number comes next in this sequence?
30 – the difference between the numbers increases by 1 each time

If I throw three coins up in the air, what is the likelihood they all land showing heads? **1 in 8 – that is, 1 in 2 times 1 in 2 times 1 in 2**

If I can type a five-letter name in 5 seconds and it takes me 6 seconds to type a six-letter name, but I can never find the W key and so it takes me three times as long to type 'W'/'w' than any other letter, which name can I type faster – Wally or Andrew? **Wally**

It takes me 15 minutes to cycle to work at 10 miles per hour. If I cycle to and from work each day, how many miles in total is my daily cycle ride? **5 miles**

If Dave's sister marries Bob's brother, what relation is Bob to Dave?
Brother-in-law

Complete the following: $99 \times 9 =$ **891** $123 \times 3 =$ **369** $72 + 71 =$ **143**

If Pete and Jane have 5 children, and each of their 5 children have 4 more children, and then half of those 4 children have 3 children of their own but the other half only have 2 children, how many great-grandchildren do Pete and Jane have?
50 great-grandchildren – they have 20 grandchildren (5×4) of which half (10) have 2 children (10×2) and half have 3 children (10×3)

Which letter comes next in this sequence?
E – alphabetical upper and lower case sequences are interleaved, two at a time from each sequence

If I weigh 80kg and pick up a kilogram of heavy potatoes, while my friend weights 81kg but picks up a kilogram of only light flowers, who now weighs the most in total? **My friend is still the heaviest**

If Tuesdays were only half the length of a normal day, how many complete weeks would there be in a year that started on a Monday given that the year would otherwise have 365 days that are each 24 hours long?
56 whole weeks – plus one day, since 365×24 = 8,760 hours in a year, divided by (6×24 + 12) = 393 days = 56 weeks and one day

How many upper-case letters look the same when reflected in a mirror?
11 – A H I M O T U V W X Y; or 10 if you write 'Y' with an angled base

If bread and milk currently cost a total of £1, of which the bread accounts for 40p, how much will the milk cost if the price goes up by 10%? **66p**

KAKURO

Instructions

Place a digit from 1 to 9 into each white square. Each horizontal run of white squares must add up to the total above the diagonal line to the left of the run, and each vertical run of white squares must add up to the total below the diagonal line above the run. **No digit can be used more than once in any run.**

Solved example

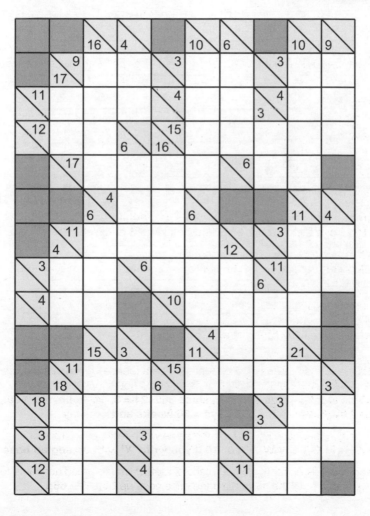

115

		\16	\4		\10	\6		\10	\9
	17\9	6	3	\3	2	1	\3	2	1
11\	8	2	1	\4	1	3	3\4	1	3
12\	9	3	6\	16\15	4	2	1	3	5
	17\	5	2	7	3	6\	2	4	
		6\4	3	1	6\			11\	4
	4\11	3	1	5	2	12\	3\	2	1
3\	1	2	6\	3	1	2	6\11	8	3
4\	3	1		10\	3	4	2	1	
		15\	3\		11\4	1	3	21\	
	18\11	9	2	6\15	2	5	1	7	3\
18\	7	2	1	3	5		3\3	2	1
3\	2	1	3\	2	1	6\	1	3	2
12\	9	3	4\	1	3	11\	2	9	

116

NURIKABE

Instructions

Shade some squares so that each number in the puzzle remains as part of a continuous unshaded area of precisely the given number of squares.

- There must be exactly one number per unshaded area.
- Shaded squares cannot form any 2×2 (or larger) areas
- All shaded squares must form one continuous area. Squares are considered to be continuous if they touch left/right/up/down, but not diagonally.

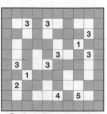

Solved example

6			3				2
							2
			1		3		
		2					2
	4						
			3		2		

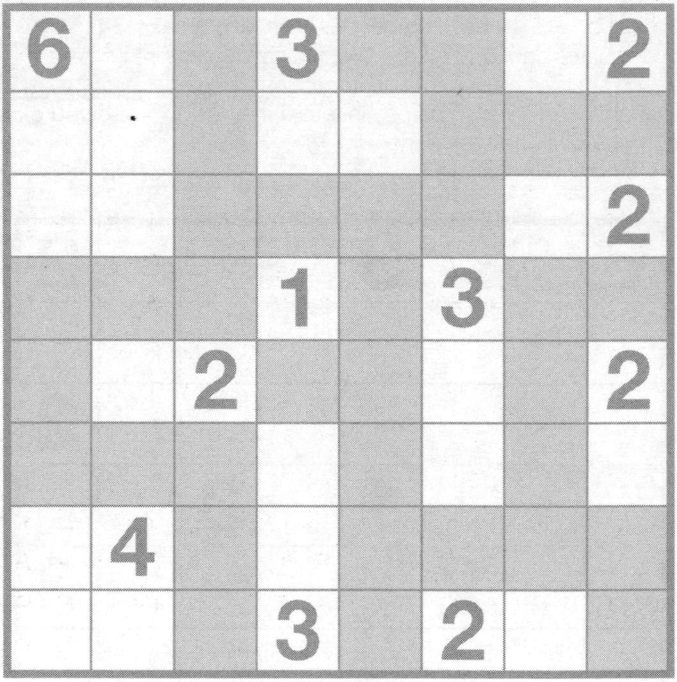

WORDSEARCH

Try to find all of the listed lakes and lochs within this wordsearch grid. Words can be written forwards or backwards in any direction, including diagonally.

O	H	C	E	E	M	S	V	N	Y	N	G	O	E	N	T
N	E	C	V	L	A	K	I	A	B	E	C	R	L	R	N
R	T	L	O	M	O	N	D	A	N	N	E	C	Y	N	W
E	E	O	K	N	S	O	A	E	S	M	C	A	N	I	T
B	I	E	S	V	N	L	V	G	S	L	A	B	E	U	D
E	N	R	P	T	L	A	H	A	A	W	S	I	M	O	E
E	T	E	O	E	A	N	R	U	I	N	O	R	L	H	V
S	O	M	N	A	T	G	G	N	R	R	A	A	I	I	N
N	R	R	B	I	Y	A	N	E	T	O	O	K	R	S	G
E	R	E	M	L	R	I	H	T	N	I	N	T	O	U	E
D	I	D	N	A	P	T	E	T	R	R	C	H	C	P	A
O	D	N	C	E	N	A	A	A	V	E	H	N	N	I	L
B	O	I	G	L	Y	H	T	K	O	P	L	Y	A	E	V
E	N	W	S	N	O	N	N	P	L	U	A	D	N	P	A
A	D	T	T	E	O	A	I	G	T	S	A	F	L	E	B
N	A	N	N	I	A	R	T	R	A	H	C	T	N	O	P

ALLEN	KATRINE	PSKOV
ANNECY	KOOTENAY	RANNOCH
BAIKAL	LINNHE	SUPERIOR
BELFAST	LOMOND	TAHOE
BODENSEE	MEECH	THIRLMERE
GENEVA	NICARAGUA	TORRIDON
GRASMERE	NYASA	VICTORIA
HURON	OKANAGAN	VOLTA
ILIAMNA	ONTARIO	WINDERMERE
ILMEN	PEIPUS	WINNIPEG
KARIBA	PONTCHARTRAIN	

MEMORY

Study this list of 25 vehicles and their locations within the grid. Take as long as you need until you feel you have memorized it. Then turn the page and fill in the grid to match as closely as you can. You will be given the first letter of each vehicle in each grid cell – the rest is up to you to remember!

Bicycle	Bus	Cab	Milk float	Taxi
Tanker	Tipper truck	Toboggan	Fire engine	Jet ski
Pram	Roadroller	Rickshaw	Aeroplane	Camper van
Coach	Train	Gritter	Scooter	Spaceship
Tandem	Tank	Unicycle	Motorbike	Van

Now try to put the vehicles back where they belong:

B	B	C	M	T
T	T	T	F	J
P	R	R	A	C
C	T	G	S	S
T	T	U	M	V

SUDOKU-X

Instructions

Place a digit from 1 to 9 in each of the empty squares in the grid, so that each row, column, bold-lined 3×3 box **and marked diagonal** contains every digit exactly once.

5	9	6	8	1	3	7	2	4
4	1	2	6	9	7	5	3	8
3	7	8	2	5	4	6	9	1
7	5	3	4	8	1	9	6	2
1	6	9	3	2	5	8	4	7
8	2	4	7	6	9	1	5	3
6	4	5	1	7	2	3	8	9
2	8	1	9	3	6	4	7	5
9	3	7	5	4	8	2	1	6

Solved example

4					5			
								9
	5				2			1
	4	6			7			
			1		8			
			4			3	5	
8			7				9	
6								
			2					7

4	6	1	9	8	5	7	2	3
7	8	2	3	1	4	5	6	9
3	5	9	6	7	2	8	4	1
2	4	6	5	3	7	9	1	8
5	9	3	1	2	8	4	7	6
1	7	8	4	9	6	3	5	2
8	2	5	7	6	3	1	9	4
6	1	7	8	4	9	2	3	5
9	3	4	2	5	1	6	8	7

Slitherlink

Draw a single loop by connecting some dots with
horizontal and vertical lines so that each numbered
square has the specified number of adjacent line
segments. The loop cannot cross or touch itself.

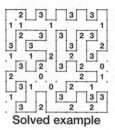

Solved example

```
3     2  3  1        3

      2              2  1

2  0        2  2  3

2     3              2

   2              2        3

   2  3  1           1  3

3  2              3

2        2  1  2     3
```

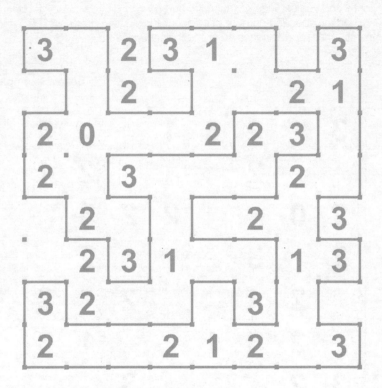

WORDSEARCH

Try to find all of the listed words, that each contain the word 'ACE', within this wordsearch grid. Words can be written forwards or backwards in any direction, including diagonally.

```
K A N Y P L A C E C A F E P Y T
Y E E C A L P S I M R F O T A O
G C K A I N T E R F A C E E E E
R A O N A E C A T S U R C C C C
I L U R A C E H O R S E A A A A
M E E N E C A F E D C L L L F L
A O C T T T L C E A U P P P R U
C H A A A R A C R F H A N K U P
E S P T F L A B E T M L O R S O
A F S R P L N C R P A A M O E P
D R O E K I A I E E T C M W R R
E E R C A R B O N A C E O U S E
A I E M G K K R C C B A C N M F
F N A S O L A C E E C L X A O A
U P I K B A C K S P A C E E T C
A D J A C E N C Y A C E T O N E
```

ACETONE
ADJACENCY
AEROSPACE
ANYPLACE
BACKSPACE
BIRTHPLACE
CARBONACEOUS
COALFACE
COMMONPLACE
CRUSTACEAN
DEFACE

DISGRACEFUL
EXACERBATE
FIREPLACE
GRIMACE
INTERFACE
MAINBRACE
MISPLACE
NECKLACE
PALACE
PEACE
POPULACE

PREFACE
RACEHORSE
RESURFACE
SHOELACE
SOLACE
TACET
TYPEFACE
UNTRACEABLE
WORKPLACE

```
K A N Y P L A C E C A F E P Y T
Y E E C A L P S I M R F O T A O
G C K A I N T E R F A C E E E E
R A O N A E C A T S U R C C C C
I L U R A C E H O R S E A A A A
M E E N E C A F E D C L L L F L
A O C T T T L C E A U P P R U
C H A A A R A C R F H A N K U P
E S P T F L A B E T M L O R S O
A F S R P L N C R P A A M O E P
D R O E K I A I E E T C M W R R
E E R C A R B O N A C E O U S E
A I E M G K K R C C B A C N M F
F N A S O L A C E E C L X A O A
U P I K B A C K S P A C E E T C
A D J A C E N C Y A C E T O N E
```

KAKURO

Instructions

Place a digit from 1 to 9 into each white square. Each horizontal run of white squares must add up to the total above the diagonal line to the left of the run, and each vertical run of white squares must add up to the total below the diagonal line above the run. **No digit can be used more than once in any run.**

Solved example

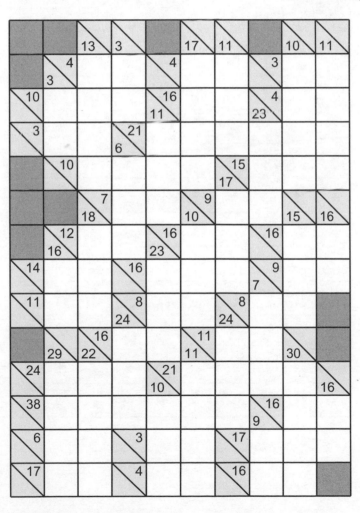

129

		13\	3\		17\	11\		10\	11\
	3\4	3	1	\4	1	3	\3	2	1
\10	1	7	2	11\16	9	7	23\4	1	3
\3	2	1	6\21	2	4	1	6	3	5
	\10	2	1	4	3	17\15	9	4	2
		18\7	2	5	10\9	1	8	15\	16\
	16\12	9	3	23\16	7	9	\16	7	9
\14	9	5	\16	8	1	7	7\9	2	7
\11	7	4	24\8	6	2	24\8	2	6	
	29\	22\16	7	9	11\11	7	4	30\	
\24	9	7	8	10\21	5	9	1	6	16\
\38	7	5	9	6	3	8	9\16	7	9
\6	5	1	\3	1	2	\17	2	8	7
\17	8	9	\4	3	1	\16	7	9	

MIXED PUZZLES

Which of these animals is the odd one out, and why?
Mouse   Frog   Newt   Toad   Salamander

Which number comes next in this sequence?
1   2   2   4   8   32   _____

In what way are these pairs of words related?
Retails and saltier   Melon and lemon   Desserts and de-stress

Which of these words would still read as a word when viewed in a mirror?
MOTTO   THAW   MOOD   TOMATO   OH

How many minutes are there in a day?

This evening I drive 10 miles from work, stop to do some shopping, then drive 15 miles home. Later on I drive 5 miles to a restaurant and then back. How far do I drive this evening?

To convert from Celsius to Fahrenheit you multiply by 9 and then divide by 5, then add 32. What is a temperature of 10°C when converted to Fahrenheit?

Complete the following:
55 + 45 + 35 = _____   99 + 89 + 79 = _____   61 + 49 − 53 = _____

How many different upper-case letters can be accurately represented on a standard 7-segment number display as found on digital watches and clocks?

Which letter comes next in this sequence?
T   W   T   F   S   _____

Complete the following:
987 + 123 = _____   55 × 4 = _____   26 × 4 = _____

If today is three days after Tuesday, and tomorrow will be five days before my birthday, what day is my birthday on?

If all vowels are replaced so that A becomes U, E becomes A, I becomes E, O becomes I and U becomes O, what unlikely occurrence is being reported in the following text? **Carry on dug perk**

If I buy some shares whose value then goes up by 10% to 88p per share, and I have 50 shares, what was the previous total value of my shares?

Which of these animals is the odd one out, and why?
Mouse – the only one that isn't an amphibian

Which number comes next in this sequence?
1   2   2   4   8   32   **256 – multiply the last two**

In what way are these pairs of words related?
The words in each pair are anagrams of one another

Which of these words would still read as a word when viewed in a mirror?
OH – it would read HO

How many minutes are there in a day?
1440 minutes

This evening I drive 10 miles from work, stop to do some shopping, then drive 15 miles home. Later on I drive 5 miles to a restaurant and then back. How far do I drive this evening?
35 miles

To convert from Celsius to Fahrenheit you multiply by 9 and then divide by 5, then add 32. What is a temperature of 10°C when converted to Fahrenheit?
50°F

Complete the following:
55 + 45 + 35 = **135**   99 + 89 + 79 = **267**   61 + 49 – 53 = **57**

How many different upper-case letters can be accurately represented on a standard 7-segment number display as found on digital watches and clocks?
13 – A C E F G H I J L O P S U (or 14 if you include Y)

Which letter comes next in this pattern?
T   W   T   F   **S – initial letters of days of the week, starting on Tuesday**

Complete the following:
987 + 123 = **1110**   55 × 4 = **220**   26 × 4 = **104**

If today is three days after Tuesday, and tomorrow will be five days before my birthday, what day is my birthday on?
Thursday

If all vowels are replaced so that A becomes U, E becomes A, I becomes E, O becomes I and U becomes O, what unlikely occurrence is being reported in the following text? **Curry in dog park**

If I buy some shares whose value then goes up by 10% to 88p per share, and I have 50 shares, what was the previous total value of my shares? **£40**

SUDOKU

Instructions

Sudoku has one very simple rule: place a digit from 1 to 9 in each of the empty squares in the grid, so that each row, column and bold-lined 3×3 box contains every digit exactly once.

9	5	3	2	7	1	6	8	4
6	2	4	3	5	8	7	1	9
8	1	7	4	6	9	3	5	2
4	9	2	7	1	3	8	6	5
1	6	8	5	9	2	4	3	7
3	7	5	6	8	4	9	2	1
5	3	9	8	2	7	1	4	6
7	8	6	1	4	5	2	9	3
2	4	1	9	3	6	5	7	8

Solved example

	3							
8				5		2	6	
9			3				5	
		4			9			1
		7		4		9		
2			1			8		
	5				6			9
	6	8		9				7
						2		

133

4	3	5	6	2	1	7	9	8
8	7	1	9	5	4	2	6	3
9	2	6	3	7	8	1	5	4
5	8	4	2	3	9	6	7	1
6	1	7	8	4	5	9	3	2
2	9	3	1	6	7	8	4	5
7	5	2	4	1	6	3	8	9
3	6	8	5	9	2	4	1	7
1	4	9	7	8	3	5	2	6

COMPREHENSION

Here's the thrilling story of five continental campers. Read this passage and then answer as many questions as you can without *checking the text again. Once you've done that, reread the text and then answer the rest.*

Bob, Dave, George, Sue and Caron decide to go camping in France. They pack themselves and everything they need into two cars and set off on the three-hour trip to the ferry, followed by the hour-long crossing and another four hours en route to the campsite. When they get to the campsite it's dark so it takes them another half an hour to find their spot. By the time they've set up their tents another two hours have passed. In the morning, they wake up to see that there are only seven other groups of people staying at the campsite.

There are three streams within an easy walk of the site. Dave and Sue decide to go off to Le Brook while the other three head off to Le Canal and Le Big River – those are the names that they decide to call them, anyway. On the way, George buys some supplies using the fifty euros he has with him, getting just five euros sixty cents in change – not enough to buy more than two cups of coffee at current camp site rates! Last year the prices were a third less.

Over the next three days they explore all five of the paths heading away from the site, with George and Caron taking over two hundred photos between them of the local flora and fauna. Bob thinks that's far too many photos; he's made do with a single roll of thirty-six on his old-school film camera.

Two days later their trip is over so they set off on the journey back; all two hundred and thirteen miles back to the ferry crossing and then one hundred and sixty miles back from the other side. It's at least ten o'clock in the evening before they're home.

- How many hours did it take after they left the ferry before they had their tents fully set up?
- How many groups of people in total were now staying at the campsite?
- What names did the group give to the three streams in the area?
- How much money did George spend on supplies on the first morning?
- How much cheaper was campsite coffee the year before?
- Which couple took over two hundred photos?
- What time was it past when they all arrived home after the holiday?
- Why did it take them a while to find their spot on arrival?
- How many cars did they take to France?
- Who was in the group of two that went off to investigate a stream on the first day?
- How many paths led away from the campsite?
- How long did the trip to the ferry take from their homes?
- What was the total distance they drove home?

How many hours did it take after they left the ferry before they had their tents fully set up?
Six and a half hours

How many groups of people in total were now staying at the campsite?
Eight, including the group in the story

What names did the group give to the three streams in the area?
Le Brook, Le Canal and Le Big River

How much money did George spend on supplies on the first morning?
Forty-four euros and forty cents

How much cheaper was campsite coffee the year before?
A third less

Which couple took over two hundred photos?
George and Caron

What time was it past when they all arrived home after the holiday?
Ten o'clock

Why did it take them a while to find their spot on arrival?
It was dark

How many cars did they take to France?
Two cars

Who was in the group of two that went off to investigate a stream on the first day?
Dave and Sue

How many paths led away from the campsite?
Five

How long did the trip to the ferry take from their homes?
Three hours

What was the total distance they drove home?
Three hundred and seventy-three miles

KAKURO

Instructions

Place a digit from 1 to 9 into each white square. Each horizontal run of white squares must add up to the total above the diagonal line to the left of the run, and each vertical run of white squares must add up to the total below the diagonal line above the run. **No digit can be used more than once in any run.**

Solved example

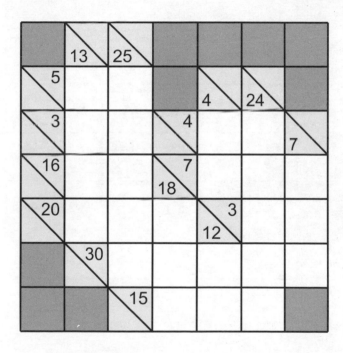

	13	25				
5	1	4		4	24	
3	2	1	4	3	1	7
16	7	9	7 / 18	1	4	2
20	3	8	9	3 / 12	2	1
	30	3	6	8	9	4
		15	3	4	8	

SHAPE COUNT

Look at the drawing below, then answer the questions that refer to it:

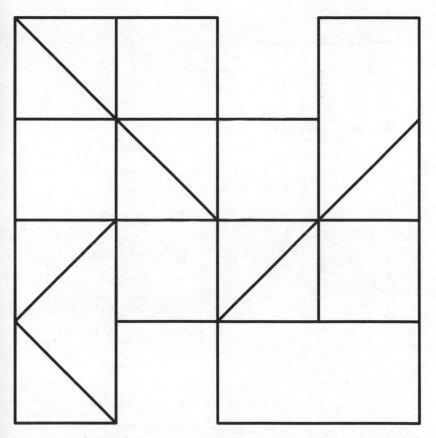

- How many right-angled triangles (◣) can you form by tracing along the lines in various ways?

- And how many squares can you form by tracing along the lines?

- What is the minimum number of straight lines that could be used to draw this illustration?

- How many rectangles, excluding squares, can you form by tracing along the lines in various ways?

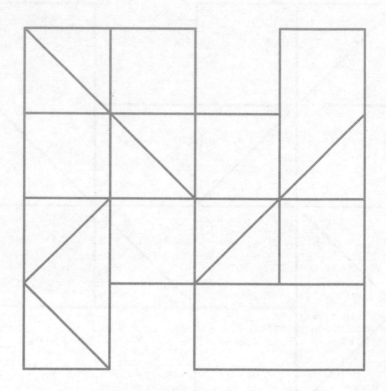

How many right-angled triangles (◣) can you form by tracing along the lines in various ways?
13

And how many squares can you form by tracing along the lines?
11

What is the minimum number of straight lines that could be used to draw this illustration?
16

How many rectangles, excluding squares, can you form by tracing along the lines in various ways?
18

MIXED PUZZLES

Which of these units is the odd one out, and why?

Mile   Acre   Kilometre   Furlong   Pint   Gallon

Which number comes next in this sequence?

7   8   9   4   5   6   _____

Right-wing is to left-wing as port is to?

Which of these numbers is divisible by 3 into a whole number?

123   302   959

How many minutes are there in twenty-three hours?

If one train leaves a station at 3:30 pm and travels at an average of 50 mph, and a second train leaves the same station at 3:45 pm but travels at an average of 60 mph, which will be first to arrive at a station 50 miles down the track?

Today is the hottest day of the year, and the coldest day was 20°C colder than this, but that cold day was still 7°C above the lowest ever recorded; today also happens to be the same margin below the hottest temperature recorded. If the hottest temperature ever recorded is 29°C, what is the lowest temperature ever recorded?

Complete the following:

13 x 12 = _____   46 x _____ = 230   246 + 357 = _____

Which letter comes next in this pattern?

A   E   F   H   I   _____

Complete the following:

0.25 x 4 = _____   Half of 940 = _____   ½ x ½ = _____

If a horse has to jump 15 fences to complete a lap of a circuit, but completes only two thirds of the course before pulling up short at a fence, given that the course consists of 2 laps how many fences did the horse jump? Assume the fences are evenly spaced around the lap and that the first fence is not precisely on the start line.

Which of these place-denoting words is not an anagram of 'retainer'?

Aretine   Eritrean   Arretine

Which of these units is the odd one out, and why?
Kilometre – the only one that is a metric measurement, not imperial

Which number comes next in this sequence?
1 – they are the numbers on a keyboard number pad reading across from left-to-right and top-to-bottom

Right-wing is to left-wing as port is to **starboard**

Which of these numbers is divisible by 3 into a whole number?
123 – if the digits of a number sum to a multiple of 3, it's a multiple of 3

How many minutes are there in twenty three hours?
1,380 minutes

If one train leaves a station at 3:30 pm and travels at an average of 50 mph, and a second train leaves the same station at 3:45 pm but travels at an average of 60 mph, which will be first to arrive at a station 50 miles down the track?
The earlier train – this will arrive at 4:30 pm; the later train at 4:35 pm

Today is the hottest day of the year, and the coldest day was 20°C colder than this, but that cold day was still 7°C above the lowest ever recorded; today also happens to be the same margin below the hottest temperature recorded. If the hottest temperature ever recorded is 29°C, what is the lowest temperature ever recorded?
-5°C

Complete the following:
13 x 12 = **156**   46 x **5** = 230   246 + 357 = **603**

Which letter comes next in this pattern?
A E F H I **K – the sequence consists of upper-case letters without any curved parts.**

Complete the following:
0.25 x 4 = **1**   Half of 940 = **470**   ½ x ½ = **¼**

If a horse has to jump 15 fences to complete a lap of a circuit, but completes only two thirds of the course before pulling up short at a fence, given that the course consists of 2 laps how many fences did the horse jump? Assume the fences are evenly spaced around the lap and that the first fence is not precisely on the start line.
19 fences

Which of these place-denoting words is not an anagram of 'retainer'?
Aretine

WORDSEARCH

Try to find all of these metals and semimetals hidden in this wordsearch grid.

```
O M M U I D A N A V U I Y N O M I T N A
N U U S O D I U M U I L L A G I H B E C
M I I N M P L A T I N U M I E O L S T E
M L R H E N I U M A R A M U R I E I S R
I L A C A D M I U M N G Z I M N A M G I
R Y M R U L B S C U E T U I A M D U N U
P R A S E O D Y M I U M A G N E S I U M
O E S M R G Y A L P I M N L I C U D T B
S B M U I S S A T O P A E M U I D R I I
M U D I C O P P E R M E O U M M B B L S
I R Y T T E R B I U M L D I U U N U T M
U E N E M R O I I E U R Y N I I I R M U
M V C T U U S N R T N I M O N D O M U T
U L M U I N I L O D A G I C A N B U I H
I I N L R M U I N E H T U R T A I I S U
R S M M U I M L O H T I M I I C U D E L
T P A L L A D I U M N O U Z T S M O A I
T H A L L I U M E C A M U I M O R H C U
Y C I N E S R A E E L N A Y R U C R E M
M U I H T I L N I C K E L H A F N I U M
```

ALUMINIUM
ANTIMONY
ARSENIC
BERYLLIUM
BISMUTH
CADMIUM
CAESIUM
CERIUM
CHROMIUM
COPPER
DYSPROSIUM
EUROPIUM
GADOLINIUM
GALLIUM
GERMANIUM
GOLD
HAFNIUM
HOLMIUM
IRIDIUM

IRON
LANTHANUM
LEAD
LITHIUM
LUTETIUM
MAGNESIUM
MANGANESE
MERCURY
MOLYBDENUM
NEODYMIUM
NICKEL
NIOBIUM
OSMIUM
PALLADIUM
PLATINUM
POTASSIUM
PRASEODYMIUM
RHENIUM
RHODIUM

RUBIDIUM
RUTHENIUM
SAMARIUM
SCANDIUM
SILVER
SODIUM
STRONTIUM
TANTALUM
TELLURIUM
THALLIUM
THORIUM
THULIUM
TITANIUM
TUNGSTEN
VANADIUM
YTTERBIUM
YTTRIUM
ZINC
ZIRCONIUM

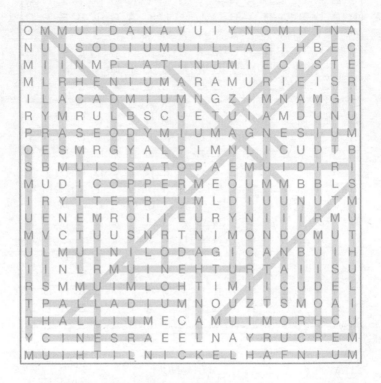

```
O M M U I D A N A V U I Y N O M I T N A
N U U S O D I U M U I L L A G I H B E C
M I I N M P L A T I N U M I E O L S T E
M L R H E N I U M A R A M U R I E I S R
I L A C A D M I U M N G Z I M N A M G I
R Y M R U L B S C U E T U I A M D U N U
P R A S E O D Y M I U M A G N E S I U M
O E S M R G Y A L P I M N L I C U D T B
S B M U I S S A T O P A E M U I D I R I
M U D I C O P P E R M E O U M M B B L S
I R Y T T E R B I U M L D I U U N U T M
U E N E M R O I I E U R Y N I I I R M U
M V C T U U S N R T N I M O N D O M U T
U L M U I N I L O D A G I C A N B U I H
I I N L R M U I N E H T U R T A I I S U
R S M M U I M L O H T I M I I C U D E L
T P A L L A D I U M N O U Z T S M O A I
T H A L L I U M E C A M U I M O R H C U
Y C I N E S R A E E L N A Y R U C R E M
M U I H T I L N I C K E L H A F N I U M
```

SLITHERLINK

Slitherlink

Draw a single loop by connecting some dots with horizontal and vertical lines so that each numbered square has the specified number of adjacent line segments. The loop cannot cross or touch itself.

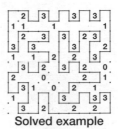

Solved example

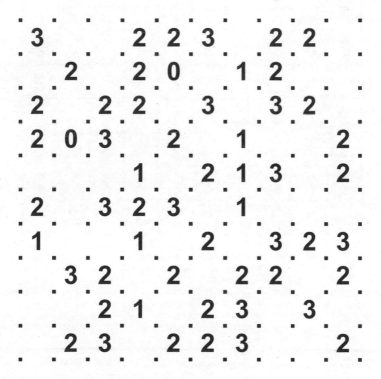

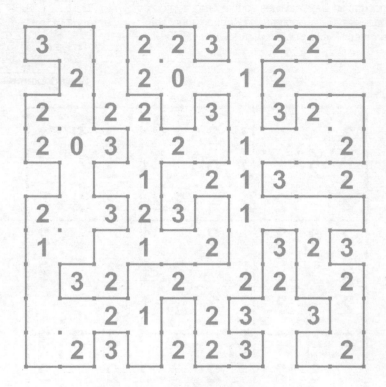

SUDOKU

Instructions

Sudoku has one very simple rule: place a digit from
1 to 9 in each of the empty squares in the grid, so that
each row, column and bold-lined 3×3 box contains
every digit exactly once.

9	5	3	2	7	1	6	8	4
6	2	4	3	5	8	7	1	9
8	1	7	4	6	9	3	5	2
4	9	2	7	1	3	8	6	5
1	6	8	5	9	2	4	3	7
3	7	5	6	8	4	9	2	1
5	3	9	8	2	7	1	4	6
7	8	6	1	4	5	2	9	3
2	4	1	9	3	6	5	7	8

Solved example

					8		3	4
				6	3		2	
				1	2		8	7
		5					4	
8								1
	7					9		
3	8		2	5				
	1		9	4				
7	4		8					

1	2	7	5	9	8	6	3	4
4	5	8	7	6	3	1	2	9
9	6	3	4	1	2	5	8	7
6	3	5	1	7	9	8	4	2
8	9	4	3	2	5	7	6	1
2	7	1	6	8	4	9	5	3
3	8	9	2	5	7	4	1	6
5	1	2	9	4	6	3	7	8
7	4	6	8	3	1	2	9	5

MEMORY

This is a tough memory challenge! Study this table, and try to remember not only the list of objects but also which box each object belongs in.

Once you think you've memorized this table as well as you can, turn the page and fill in the empty grid as accurately as possible.

Mobile phone	Pen	Television	Front door	Cranberry
Pencil	Desk	Tree bark	Book	Skipping rope
Eagle	Silver birch	Fence post	Orange	Tricycle
Trumpet	Tablet computer	USB cable	Bicycle	Car
Walnut	Lemonade	Dressing gown	Poster	Map
Yacht	Telegraph pole	Voting paper	Globe	SIM card

See if you can recall all 30 objects, and where they went:

KAKURO

Instructions

Place a digit from 1 to 9 into each white square. Each horizontal run of white squares must add up to the total above the diagonal line to the left of the run, and each vertical run of white squares must add up to the total below the diagonal line above the run. **No digit can be used more than once in any run.**

Solved example

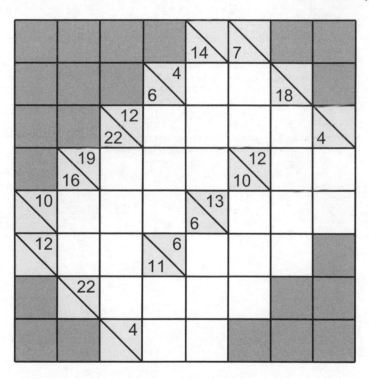

				14\	7\		
			4\ 6\	**3**	**1**	18\	
		12\ 22\	**3**	**2**	**6**	**1**	4\
	19\ 16\	**8**	**2**	**9**	12\ 10\	**9**	**3**
10\	**7**	**2**	**1**	13\ 6\	**7**	**5**	**1**
12\	**9**	**3**	6\ 11\	**2**	**1**	**3**	
	22\	**9**	**8**	**3**	**2**		
		4\	**3**	**1**			

MIXED PUZZLES

Which of these words is the odd one out, and why?
Earth   **Moon**   **Wind**   **Fire**   **Water**

Which number comes next in this sequence?
1   4   9   16   ___

Which of these words does not fit with the rest?
Levier   Relive   Virile   Revile

If I fall asleep at 10:30 pm and wake up at 6:15 pm, how long have I been asleep?

If Sue drives at 60 mph for 10 minutes, then 30 mph for 10 minutes followed by 70 mph for 6 minutes, how far does she travel in those 26 minutes?

If Sydney's summer time clock is 11 hours ahead of the UK while it's winter in the UK, how many hours ahead of the UK is Sydney when it's summer in the UK, given that both countries move their clocks forward an hour for the summer but back again in the winter?

Complete the following:
35% of 200 = ___   95% of 500 = ___   20% of 10% of 100 = ___

My sister's uncle's wife's daughter's brother is my cousin – true or false?

Which letter comes next in this sequence?
O   T   T   F   F   S   S   ___

Complete the following:
50 – 60 + 30 = ___   99 – 199 + 299 = ___   3 × 7 × 5 = ___

If I press the button '4' on my mobile phone I select G, then H, then I, while when I press '8' I get T, then U, then V. How many key presses do I need to type 'THIGH'?

Which of these word pairs are not homophones? (Homophones are words that sound the same but are spelled differently).
Aural & Oral   Write & Right   Bread & Breed   Altar & Alter

True or false – if you put your right hand on your left ear and your left hand in your left pocket then if you look a mirror you'll see that your right ear is being held by your left hand and your right hand is in your left pocket?

Which of these words is the odd one out, and why?
Moon – the only one that isn't an ancient element

Which number comes next in this sequence?
25 – they are square numbers in increasing order, 1×1, 2×2, 3×3, etc

Which of these words does not fit with the rest?
Virile – the other three are anagrams of one another

If I fall asleep at 10:30 pm and wake up at 6:15 pm how long have I been asleep?
7 hours 45 minutes

If Sue drives at 60 mph for 10 minutes, then 30 mph for 10 minutes followed by 70 mph for 6 minutes, how far does she travel in those 26 minutes?
22 miles

If Sydney's summer time clock is 11 hours ahead of the UK while it's winter in the UK, how many hours ahead of the UK is Sydney when it's summer in the UK, given that both countries move their clocks forward an hour for the summer but back again in the winter?
9 hours ahead

Complete the following:
35% of 200 = **70**   95% of 500 = **475**   20% of 10% of 100 = **2**

My sister's uncle's wife's daughter's brother is my cousin – true or false?
True

Which letter comes next in this sequence?
O T T F F S S **E – the initials of One, Two, Three, Four, etc**

Complete the following:
50 – 60 + 30 = **20**   99 – 199 + 299 = **199**   3 × 7 × 5 = **105**

If I press the button '4' on my mobile phone I select G, then H, then I, while when I press '8' I get T, then U, then V. How many key presses do I need to type 'THIGH'?
9 key presses

Which of these word pairs are not homophones? (Homophones are words that sound the same but are spelled differently).
Bread & Breed

True or false – if you put your right hand on your left ear and your left hand in your left pocket then if you look a mirror you'll see that your right ear is being held by your left hand and your right hand is in your left pocket?
False – it will appear your hand is in your right pocket

WORDSEARCH

Try to find all of these musical instruments hidden within this wordsearch grid.

```
O B O E N I R U O B M A T E I A B B R M
F G N C B K E T T L E D R U M O A M E U
R U U A T D Z S T C C V U P D N N O C I
E H U S P A I I A R L I I H J I I N O N
N E A T L L S D W C L A R O S I T A R O
C N E A O A E T G L A A V N L U R I D M
H O L N Z M H E E E N R C I B A E P E R
H H T E T H T A T E R S A U C O C D R A
O P S T I L N O L S H I L M S H N N M H
R A I S I P Y T M T A A D N A F O A U R
N S H E I M S R E U R L E O X L C R R A
A U W P T I P N E B P G N O O U I G D I
G O E E H E I A E A S N O S P G A U E N
R S E W R P N L N K I A H S H E L I R S
O F N L S H L O A I C R P A O L B T A T
H I A C G S U G R A H O O B N H A A N I
T F W N E U A N E D O C L O E O T R S C
U E S A L L B O H U R D Y G U R D Y C K
O S S A B E L B U O D U X I G N A R A S
M M N O I D R O C C A B M E L O D E O N
```

ACCORDION
BANJO
BASSOON
BODHRAN
BONGO
BUGLE
CASTANETS
CELLO
CLAVICHORD
CONCERTINA
COR ANGLAIS
CRWTH
DIDGERIDOO
DOUBLE BASS
ERHU
EUPHONIUM
FIFE
FLUGELHORN
FRENCH HORN

GLOCKENSPIEL
GRAND PIANO
GUITAR
GUSLA
HARMONIUM
HARPSICHORD
HURDY-GURDY
KETTLEDRUM
LYRE
MARACAS
MELODEON
MOUTH ORGAN
OBOE
OUD
RAINSTICK
RECORDER
SARANGI
SAXOPHONE
SAZ

SITAR
SNARE DRUM
SOUSAPHONE
SPINET
STEEL PAN
SWANEE WHISTLE
SYNTHESIZER
TABLA
TAMBOURINE
TENOR DRUM
TIMPANI
TIN WHISTLE
TOM-TOM
TUBA
TUBULAR BELLS
UILLEAN PIPES
VIOLA
XYLOPHONE

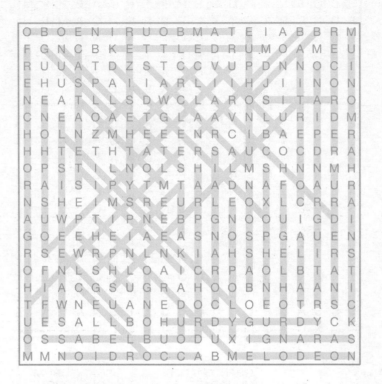

```
O B O E N I R U O B M A T E I A B B R M
F G N C B K E T T L E D R U M O A M E U
R U U A T D Z S T C C V U P D N N O C I
E H U S P A I I A R L I I H J I I N O N
N E A T L L S D W C L A R O S I T A R O
C N E A O A E T G L A A V N L U R I D M
H O L N Z M H E E E N R C I B A E P E R
H H T E T H T A T E R S A U C O C D R A
O P S T I L N O L S H I L M S H N N M H
R A I S I P Y T M T A A D N A F O A U R
N S H E I M S R E U R L E O X L C R R A
A U W P T I P N E B P G N O O U I G D I
G O E E H E I A E A S N O S P G A U E N
R S E W R P N L N K I A H S H E L I R S
O F N L S H L O A I C R P A O L B T A T
H I A C G S U G R A H O O B N H A A N I
T F W N E U A N E D O C L O E O T R S C
U E S A L L B O H U R D Y G U R D Y C K
O S S A B E L B U O D U X I G N A R A S
M M N O I D R O C C A B M E L O D E O N
```

SUDOKU

Instructions

Sudoku has one very simple rule: place a digit from 1 to 9 in each of the empty squares in the grid, so that each row, column and bold-lined 3×3 box contains every digit exactly once.

9	5	3	2	7	1	6	8	4
6	2	4	3	5	8	7	1	9
8	1	7	4	6	9	3	5	2
4	9	2	7	1	3	8	6	5
1	6	8	5	9	2	4	3	7
3	7	5	6	8	4	9	2	1
5	3	9	8	2	7	1	4	6
7	8	6	1	4	5	2	9	3
2	4	1	9	3	6	5	7	8

Solved example

	7	2	6	8	1			
	1			7		8		
						3		
		4	6					
	3	2				8	5	
				4	9			
	2							
	5		1				7	
		1	5	3	9	4		

3	9	7	2	6	8	1	4	5
5	1	6	3	4	7	2	8	9
2	4	8	9	1	5	6	3	7
9	8	4	6	5	3	7	1	2
6	3	2	7	9	1	8	5	4
1	7	5	8	2	4	9	6	3
8	2	3	4	7	6	5	9	1
4	5	9	1	8	2	3	7	6
7	6	1	5	3	9	4	2	8

Dave's decided to write some melodramatic poetry. It took him at least five minutes. Read it once, then answer as many questions as you can without checking back. Then read it again before answering the rest.

REGRET

Seven months have softly flowed;
Time has twisted, wound and weaved.
Another year of absent crew,
Left unchallenged. Run right through.

Nine and three the years untold;
Wandered freely, flags unfurled.
Wind that doesn't wave the tree;
Losing nightly. Scaring me.

Flowers miss their springtime cheer,
Waters boundless wait and ebb.
Caught in pasts so deeply bound;
Left behind. And never found.

Grasping hands have missed their bar;
Muddled frenzies face the past,
And chase it down, then turn away –
Space engulfed. Wild affray.

Immolation wears the crown,
Of fought and battled, torn and won.
Lost and searching, shorn of time;
Sheep not cattle. No life, no rhyme.

- How many years does Dave describe as 'untold'?
- What body parts apparently missed their 'bar'?
- What is wrong with the flowers now?
- How many verses start with a number?
- What was disturbing about the tree in Dave's poem?
- What animal is present instead of cattle?
- What period of time flowed 'softly'?
- What was 'boundless' and waiting?
- What is special about the last two lines of each verse?
- Some things were 'unfurled' – what were they?
- What did the 'muddled frenzies' face?
- The final line of each verse always has how many full stops?
- At least how long did it take Dave to write the poem?
- What is the poem called?

SOLUTION

Exercise 74 ◊ Expert

How many years does Dave describe as 'untold'?
Twelve years

What body parts apparently missed their 'bar'?
Hands

What is wrong with the flowers now?
They miss their springtime cheer

How many verses start with a number?
Two

What was disturbing about the tree in Dave's poem?
The wind didn't affect it

What animal is present instead of cattle?
Sheep

What period of time flowed 'softly'?
Seven months

What was 'boundless' and waiting?
Waters

What is special about the last two lines of each verse?
They always rhyme

Some things were 'unfurled' – what were they?
A flag

What did the 'muddled frenzies' face?
The past

The final line of each verse always has how many full stops?
Two

At least how long did it take Dave to write the poem?
Five minutes

What is the poem called?
Regret

SLITHERLINK

Slitherlink

Draw a single loop by connecting some dots with horizontal and vertical lines so that each numbered square has the specified number of adjacent line segments. The loop cannot cross or touch itself.

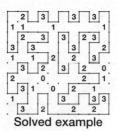

Solved example

```
  2       3 1     2

3 3 2         3 1 1

          3       2 1 3

3 2     1 2 0 1 3 2 2

2   2       2   2 1

  1 2   2       2   2

3 2 2 2 2 1 3     1 2

2 3 2         2

  2 0 2           1 1 2

  3         2 3     3
```

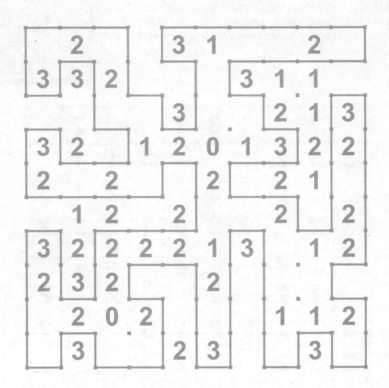

Exercise 76 ◊ Expert

KAKURO

Instructions

Place a digit from 1 to 9 into each white square. Each horizontal run of white squares must add up to the total above the diagonal line to the left of the run, and each vertical run of white squares must add up to the total below the diagonal line above the run. **No digit can be used more than once in any run.**

Solved example

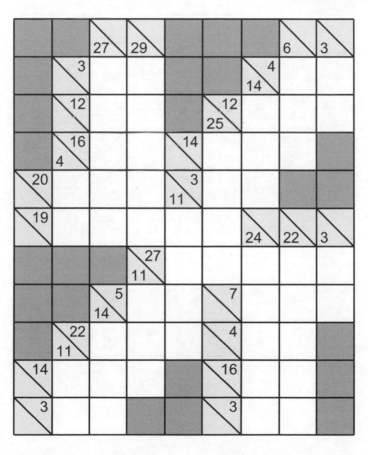

163

		27\	29\				6\	3\
	\3	1	2			14\4	3	1
	\12	4	8		25\12	9	1	2
	4\16	9	7	\14	9	3	2	
\20	3	8	9	11\3	1	2		
\19	1	5	3	2	8	24\	22\	3\
			11\27	1	7	8	9	2
		14\5	2	3	\7	4	2	1
	11\22	9	8	5	\4	1	3	
\14	9	4	1		\16	9	7	
\3	2	1			\3	2	1	

MIXED PUZZLES

Which of these musical instruments is the odd one out, and why?
Trumpet   Clarinet   Trombone   French horn   Tuba

Which number comes next in this sequence?
1   3   9   27   81   _____

Can you find the connection between all these words?
Whine   Rhumb   Coax   Jinn

Think of a number. Add 26. Multiply by 90. Divide by 180. Multiply by 2. Subtract the number you thought of to start with. What is the result?

If every hour had only 50 minutes, how many minutes shorter would a day be?

If I drive at 30 mph for 6 minutes, then 60 mph for 10 minutes, followed by 30 mph for 4 minutes, what is my average speed over those 20 minutes?

To convert from Celsius (C) to Kelvin (K) you add 273.15. If it's 26°C outside right now, which is 9°K cooler than the hottest it's been today, what is today's hottest temperature in Kelvin?

Complete the following:
10% of 50% = _____   Half of a third of a quarter = _____   50 x 45 = _____

If an elephant never forgets and it learns 4 facts a day, how many facts does it learn in a 4-year period, assuming a leap year once every 4 years?

Which letter comes next in this sequence?
W   L   C   N   I   T   _____

Complete the following:
77 x 11 = _____   5 x 98 = _____   103 + 484 = _____

If a perfectly flat and square island has a surface area of 8,100 square metres, how wide is the island at its narrowest?

How many of these words have more consonants than vowels?
Separately   Extremely   Confusing   Muddled   Failure

If I'm happy exactly 90% of the time, but when I sleep I'm always happy, what percentage of the time am I both awake and not happy?

SOLUTION

Exercise 77 ◊ Expert

Which of these musical instruments is the odd one out, and why?
Clarinet – only one that isn't a brass instrument

Which number comes next in this sequence?
243 – each number is 3 times the previous number

Can you find the connection between all these words?
They are all homophones of drinks – wine, rum, cokes and gin

Think of a number. Add 26. Multiply by 90. Divide by 180. Multiply by 2.
Subtract the number you thought of to start with. What is the result?
26 – most of the sequence cancels itself out

If every hour had only 50 minutes, how many minutes shorter would a day be?
240 minutes shorter

If I drive at 30 mph for 6 minutes, then 60 mph for 10 minutes, followed by 30
mph for 4 minutes, what is my average speed over those 20 minutes?
**I travel 3 miles, 10 miles and 2 miles respectively in 20 minutes, so my
average speed is 45 mph**

To convert from Celsius (C) to Kelvin (K) you add 273.15. If it's 26°C outside
right now, which is 9°K cooler than the hottest it's been today, what is today's
hottest temperature in Kelvin? **308.15°K**

Complete the following:
10% of 50% = **5%**   Half of a third of a quarter = **A twenty-fourth**
50 x 45 = **2250**

If an elephant never forgets and it learns 4 facts a day, how many facts does it
learn in a 4-year period, assuming a leap year once every 4 years?
5844 facts – clever elephant!

Which letter comes next in this sequence?
W L C N I T **S – it is the first letter of the words in the question!**

Complete the following:
77 x 11 = **847**   5 x 98 = **490**   103 + 484 = **587**

If a perfectly flat and square island has a surface area of 8,100 square metres,
how wide is the island at its narrowest? **90 metres wide**

How many of these words have more consonants than vowels?
4 – all of them except 'failure'

If I'm happy exactly 90% of the time, but when I sleep I'm always happy, what
percentage of the time am I both awake and not happy?
10% of the time

MEMORY

This grid contains 30 types of government. On the next page see if you can recall where all 30 went. You will be given a list of the 30 types but all of the boxes will be empty.

Heptarchy	Monarchy	Tyranny	Democracy	Constitutionalism
Ergatocracy	Absolutism	Communalism	Triarchy	Slavocracy
Squirearchy	Gerontocracy	Hierocracy	Meritocracy	Imperialism
Anarchy	Arlstocracy	Plutocracy	Hexarchy	Isocracy
Oligarchy	Pantisocracy	Quangocracy	Technocracy	Hagiocracy
Dictatorship	Corporatism	Bureaucracy	Ochlocracy	Nomocracy

Try to put the governmental types back in the grid, but note that there's one extra type added into the list that doesn't belong in any of the boxes.

Anarchy	absence of government
Aristocracy	by nobility
Absolutism	by an absolute ruler
Bureaucracy	by officials
Communalism	by self-governing communities
Corporatism	by corporations
Constitutionalism	by constitution
Dictatorship	by a dictator
Democracy	by the people
Ergatocracy	by the workers
Gerontocracy	by old people
Hierocracy	by priests
Hexarchy	by six rulers
Heptarchy	by seven rulers
Hagiocracy	by holy men
Isocracy	by equals
Imperialism	by emperor/empire
Meritocracy	by merit
Monarchy	by monarch
Nomocracy	by rule of law
Oligarchy	by the few
Ochlocracy	by mob
Pantisocracy	by all equally
Plutocracy	by the rich
Ptochocracy	by the poor
Quangocracy	by quangos
Squirearchy	by squires
Slavocracy	by slaveholders
Tyranny	by a tyrant
Technocracy	by experts
Triarchy	by three rulers

WORDSEARCH

Try to find all of these colours that have been hidden in this wordsearch grid.

```
E N L P A N H M I L L A F L E R T G T R
A L R I C A B R O W N T S T O G A R H C
A O E A G A I E T I H W C S I B F D B N
B T A B J R U B Y N O B E O A L L I R R
E G N A R O E M I L R P J N W A F M A N
I F A Z C O R A L L I N A V R P A R A M
G I Y U A T N E G A M A S E R R V V A T
E O C R S N Y Z V A V M M G O I O G S E
H L U E G G S H E L L E I O O C N Y B N
H I V S R F O R D C I R N L A O H I U A
Y V D H A U C C N A Q S E D L T U L S I
E E F F O C L H H R U T O I E U T A N E
R V S D Z H E E A M O U A M A R A N T H
G C S H Y S L S A I R C A I A Q E S H S
E L A I C I C T E N I R A M A U Q A E V
D I R E E A S N C E C H A R C O A L H E
A U B U R N T U M B E R T Y S I S M J O
J C A L I L N T E R I H P P A S O O W A
E I E B S G P A I N D I G O A E G N A N
S T S I E G R E E N G A P M A H C D C N
```

ALMOND	CHESTNUT	LIQUORICE
AMARANTH	COFFEE	MAGENTA
AMBER	CORAL	MAGNOLIA
AMETHYST	CORN	MAROON
APRICOT	CREAM	OLIVE
AQUAMARINE	CYAN	ORANGE
AUBURN	EBONY	ROSE
AVOCADO	EGGSHELL	RUBY
AZURE	EMERALD	SALMON
BEIGE	FAWN	SAPPHIRE
BLUE	FUCHSIA	SCARLET
BRASS	GOLD	SEPIA
BRONZE	GREEN	SIENNA
BROWN	GREY	SILVER
BURNT UMBER	INDIGO	TURQUOISE
CARMINE	JADE	ULTRAMARINE
CERISE	JASMINE	VANILLA
CERULEAN	LAVENDER	VIOLET
CHAMPAGNE	LILAC	WHITE
CHARCOAL	LIME	YELLOW

```
E N L P A N H M I L L A F L E R T G T R
A L R I C A B R O W N T S T O G A R H C
A O E A G A I E T I H W C S I B F D B N
B T A B J R U B Y N O B E O A L L I R R
E G N A R O E M I L R P J N W A F M A N
I F A Z C O R A L L I N A V R P A R A M
G I Y U A T N E G A M A S E R R V V A T
E O C R S N Y Z V A V M M G O I O G S E
H L U E G G S H E L L E I O O C N Y B N
H I V S R F O R D C I R N L A O H I U A
Y V D H A U C C N A Q S E D L T U L S I
E E F F O C L H H R U T O I E U T A N E
R V S D Z H E E A M O U A M A R A N T H
G C S H Y S L S A I R C A I A Q E S H S
E L A I C I C T E N I R A M A U Q A E V
D I R E E A S N C E C H A R C O A L H E
A U B U R N T U M B E R T Y S I S M J O
J C A L I L N T E R I H P P A S O O W A
E I E B S G P A I N D I G O A E G N A N
S T S I E G R E E N G A P M A H C D C N
```

KILLER SUDOKU

Instructions

Place a digit from 1 to 9 in each of the empty squares in the grid, so that each row, column and bold-lined 3×3 box contains every digit exactly once. The content of each dashed-line cage must sum to the total given at the top-left of that cage. You **cannot repeat** a number within a cage.

6	1	9	2	4	7	3	8	5
5	4	3	1	6	8	2	9	7
7	2	8	5	3	9	4	1	6
2	9	7	4	5	1	6	3	8
4	8	6	9	7	3	5	2	1
3	5	1	6	8	2	7	4	9
8	7	5	3	9	4	1	6	2
9	3	2	7	1	6	8	5	4
1	6	4	8	2	5	9	7	3

Solved example

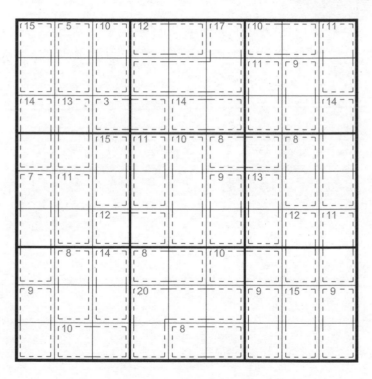

171

8	2	4	5	7	3	9	1	6
7	3	6	4	9	1	8	2	5
5	9	1	2	6	8	3	7	4
9	4	7	8	5	6	2	3	1
1	6	8	3	4	2	7	5	9
2	5	3	9	1	7	6	4	8
4	7	5	6	2	9	1	8	3
3	1	9	7	8	4	5	6	2
6	8	2	1	3	5	4	9	7

MIXED PUZZLES

Which of these fruits is the odd one out, and why?
Apple   Orange   Cherry   Fig   Tomato

Sorts these numbers into the alphabetical order of their corresponding words:
1   2   4   5   3   9

What number comes next in this sequence?
31   28   31   30   _____

If the printer sends me 10% more business cards than I ordered, and after a year I have 25% left of those I had from the printer, how many did I order originally if I now have 275 cards left?

Given that a millisecond is a thousandth of a second, how many milliseconds are there in a minute?

If I drive the 40 miles from Cardiff to Swansea at 60 mph, but my friend catches the train that takes a 30-mile route but stops at lots of stations and goes an average of only 40 mph, who will arrive first if we both leave at the same time?

If the hottest country in the world today is Egypt, which is twice as hot in degrees Celsius as Japan, which in turn is three times hotter than Greenland, how hot is it in Iceland if it's three degrees cooler than a fifth of the temperature of Greenland and it's thirty Celsius in Egypt?

Complete the following:
0.5 x 25 = _____   50 x 350 = _____   80 x 700 = _____

If somebody born on the 13th March 1878 died on the 2nd January 1953, how many birthdays had they celebrated by the time they died?

Which letter comes next in this pattern: **A   S   D   F   G   _____**

Complete the following:
Half of 80% of a third of 300 = _____   9 x 8 x 7 x 6 x 4 x 2 = _____

What is the sum of all numbers less than 50 that contain the digit '1'?

If I've completed half of the 'mixed puzzles' pages in this book up to this page, including this one, how many of these pages do I have left to complete?

SOLUTION

Which of these fruits is the odd one out, and why?
Tomato – the only one that doesn't grow on a tree

Sorts these numbers into the alphabetical order of their corresponding words:
5, 4, 9, 1, 3, 2 – Five, Four, Nine, One, Three, Two

What number comes next in this sequence?
31 – the number of days normally in January, February, March, etc

If the printer sends me 10% more business cards than I ordered, and after a year I have 25% left of those I had from the printer, how many did I order originally if I now have 275 cards left? **1,000 cards**

Given that a millisecond is a thousandth of a second, how many milliseconds are there in a minute? **60,000 milliseconds**

If I drive the 40 miles from Cardiff to Swansea at 60 mph, but my friend catches the train that takes a 30-mile route but stops at lots of stations and goes an average of only 40 mph, who will arrive first if we both leave at the same time?
I will – my car journey takes me 40 minutes, but my friend's train journey takes them 45 minutes

If the hottest country in the world today is Egypt, which is twice as hot in degrees Celsius as Japan, which in turn is three times hotter than Greenland, how hot is it in Iceland if it's three degrees cooler than a fifth of the temperature of Greenland and it's thirty Celsius in Egypt? **-2°C (in Iceland)**

Complete the following:
0.5 x 25 = **12.5**   50 x 350 = **17500**   80 x 700 = **56000**

If somebody born on the 13th March 1878 died on the 2nd January 1953, how many birthdays had they celebrated by the time they died?
74 birthdays

Which letter comes next in this pattern?
H – the letters on a standard QWERTY keyboard, reading from left to right across the middle row

Complete the following:
Half of 80% of a third of 300 = **40**   9 x 8 x 7 x 6 x 4 x 2 = **24192**

What is the sum of all numbers less than 50 that contain the digit '1'?
239 – i.e. 1+10+11+...+18+19+21+31+41

If I've completed half of the 'mixed puzzles' pages in this book up to this page, including this one, how many of these pages do I have left to complete?
8 pages – this is the 14th page of 15 in total, so I have done 7 so far

KAKURO

Instructions

Place a digit from 1 to 9 into each white square. Each horizontal run of white squares must add up to the total above the diagonal line to the left of the run, and each vertical run of white squares must add up to the total below the diagonal line above the run. **No digit can be used more than once in any run.**

Solved example

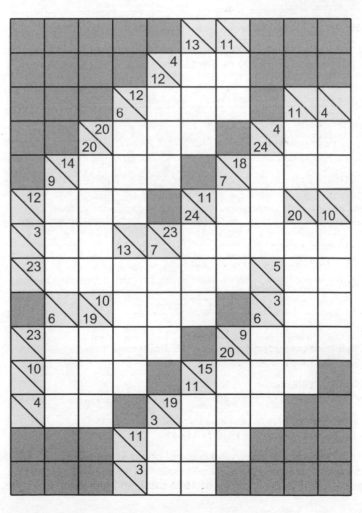

Kakuro solution grid:

					13\	11\			
				4\12	**1**	**3**			
			12\6	**1**	**3**	**8**		11\	4\
		20\20	**3**	**8**	**9**	4\24		**3**	**1**
	14\9	**9**	**2**	**3**		18\7	**7**	**8**	**3**
12\	**3**	**8**	**1**		11\24	**2**	**9**	20\	10\
3\	**1**	**2**	13\	23\7	**9**	**1**	**8**	**3**	**2**
23\	**5**	**1**	**3**	**2**	**8**	**4**	5\	**1**	**4**
6\	10\19	**2**	**1**	**7**		3\6	**2**	**1**	
23\	**3**	**9**	**7**	**4**		9\20	**1**	**5**	**3**
10\	**2**	**7**	**1**	15\11	**4**	**2**	**9**		
4\	**1**	**3**		19\3	**7**	**9**	**3**		
			11\	**1**	**3**	**7**			
			3\	**2**	**1**				

NURIKABE

Instructions

Shade some squares so that each number in the puzzle remains as part of a continuous unshaded area of precisely the given number of squares.

- There must be exactly one number per unshaded area.
- Shaded squares cannot form any 2×2 (or larger) areas
- All shaded squares must form one continuous area. Squares are considered to be continuous if they touch left/right/up/down, but not diagonally.

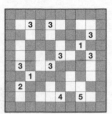

Solved example

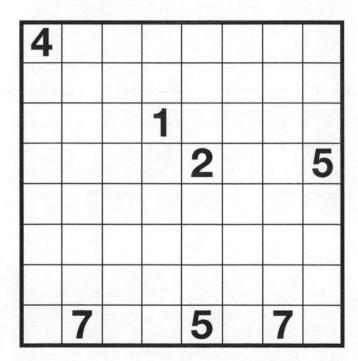

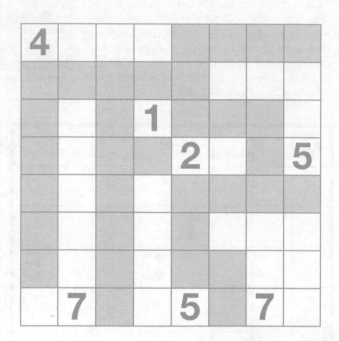

WORDSEARCH

Try to find all of these words starting "AB" hidden within this wordsearch grid.

```
A M T S A E R B A Y L L A M R O N B A T
I E T B B L I E S B A B A T T O I R A A
O A D N R E L B A B S C O N D D A B B N
T B L T A B A S H O I O A Y I A L J A A
N O T L S R H N L S I D R B A U E R C B
A R N N I M R U A R N T I P S C R D U O
Y A E D O S T E R U J B A H T E T L S U
E L B A N I M O B A B O R I G I N A L T
B R R B O T T A L A M S Y B A O O T N S
A I O N Y U O A N A I O D B I R I N E S
B R S E A L T B C A B O R T T S T C M E
O B B G E O N B B I E I A B O U N D O C
T B A A B S U R D A D G O D E A E E D S
A J B T D B O E R G O B B T R N T S B B
N N O I T A I V E R B B A R O U S A A A
T O L O D E C I B D A G E L L A B B B B
Y N I N O I T A R R E B A O E B A A D R
U T S E L B A T R N A B S T R A C T U U
A C H E I S S E B B A B A N D O N E C P
C B J N E E D A R B A B I L I T Y U T T
```

ABACUS	ABILITY	ABRASION
ABALONE	ABJECT	ABREAST
ABANDON	ABJURE	ABRIDGE
ABASE	ABLER	ABROAD
ABASH	ABLEST	ABROGATION
ABATE	ABLUSH	ABRUPT
ABATTOIR	ABNEGATE	ABSCESS
ABBESS	ABNEGATION	ABSCOND
ABBEY	ABNORMALLY	ABSEIL
ABBOT	ABOARD	ABSENTEE
ABBREVIATE	ABODE	ABSOLUTE
ABBREVIATION	ABOLISH	ABSOLUTION
ABDICATION	ABOMINABLE	ABSOLUTISM
ABDOMEN	ABORAL	ABSORBENT
ABDUCT	ABORIGINAL	ABSORPTION
ABED	ABORT	ABSTENTION
ABERRANCE	ABOUND	ABSTRACT
ABERRANT	ABOUT	ABSURD
ABERRATION	ABRACADABRA	ABUNDANT
ABEYANT	ABRADE	ABYSMAL

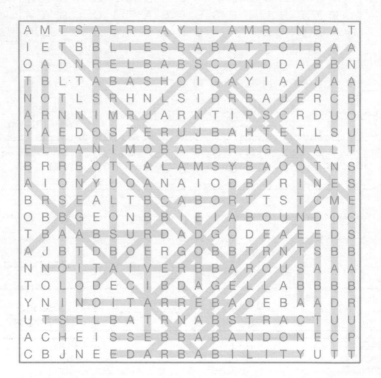

A M T S A E R B A Y L L A M R O N B A T
I E T B B L I E S B A B A T T O I R A A
O A D N R E L B A B S C O N D D A B B N
T B L T A B A S H O I O A Y I A L J A A
N O T L S R H N L S I D R B A U E R C B
A R N N I M R U A R N T I P S C R D U O
Y A E D O S T E R U J B A H T E T L S U
E L B A N I M O B A B O R I G I N A L T
B R R B O T T A L A M S Y B A O O T N S
A I O N Y U O A N A I O D B I R I N E S
B R S E A L T B C A B O R T T S T C M E
O B B G E O N B B I E I A B O U N D O C
T B A A B S U R D A D G O D E A E E D S
A J B T D B O E R G O B B T R N T S B B
N N O I T A I V E R B B A R O U S A A A
T O L O D E C I B D A G E L L A B B B B
Y N I N O I T A R R E B A O E B A A D R
U T S E L B A T R N A B S T R A C T U U
A C H E I S S E B B A B A N D O N E C P
C B J N E E D A R B A B I L I T Y U T T

MEMORY

Try to remember where these 24 historical characters have been placed in the table, then write them back in on the next page. You won't be given any of the names – you'll have to recall them all! Good luck!

Alexander the Great	Martin Luther	Mahatma Gandhi	Socrates
Marco Polo	Napoleon Bonaparte	Geronimo	George Washington
Boudicca	Guy Fawkes	Attila the Hun	Henry VIII
Billy the Kid	Leon Trotsky	Robert the Bruce	Joseph Stalin
Winston Churchill	Horatio Nelson	Julius Caesar	Charlemagne
Davy Crockett	Walter Raleigh	Yuri Gagarin	Florence Nightingale

Now try to write them back in – just a few first letters are given:

	M		
		G	
			H
B			
	H		
		Y	

KILLER SUDOKU

Instructions

Place a digit from 1 to 9 in each of the empty squares in the grid, so that each row, column and bold-lined 3×3 box contains every digit exactly once. The content of each dashed-line cage must sum to the total given at the top-left of that cage. You **cannot repeat** a number within a cage.

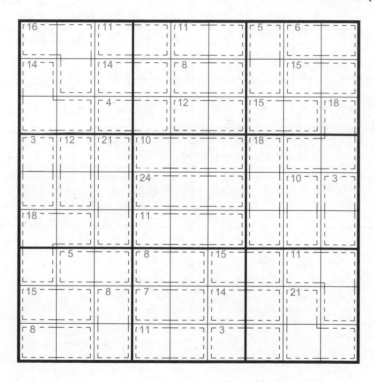

Solved example

183

6	9	7	4	8	3	2	1	5
4	1	5	9	2	6	3	8	7
8	2	3	1	7	5	9	6	4
2	7	8	3	6	1	4	5	9
1	5	4	8	9	7	6	3	2
3	6	9	2	5	4	8	7	1
9	4	1	5	3	8	7	2	6
7	8	2	6	1	9	5	4	3
5	3	6	7	4	2	1	9	8

SLITHERLINK

Slitherlink

Draw a single loop by connecting some dots with
horizontal and vertical lines so that each numbered
square has the specified number of adjacent line
segments. The loop cannot cross or touch itself.

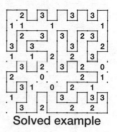

Solved example

```
1 2    1 2 3    2
  3            1    2
2   0    1 3            2
2 2 3 2      0 2 2 1
1   2          1
      2            2    1
3 2 3 1      2 2 3 3
1          2 3    3    2
  2    2          2
  1    3 3 3    1 2
```

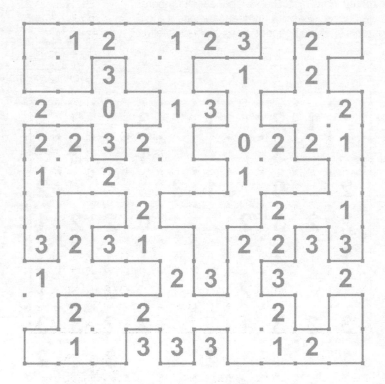

WORDSEARCH

Try to find all of these countries that have been hidden in this wordsearch grid.

```
A K A R G E N T I N A T U H B D S Z C K
U Y A T A S U R I N A M E C N A R F O L
N R S P U C A M B O D I A A I R E G L A
O G U Y Y E S R E J A O L A G U T R O P
C Y R G A U G A R A C I N N A A S S M A
H Z A E U R E P G E Z I L E B U Y P B K
I S L G E A S O M A L I A A S G R A I I
L T E K A N Y O W O D A N A R I I I A S
E A B D L W L S K A Z A K H S T A N N T
L N T H A I L A N D T A M U L N S A S A
P S B D M L B F N S I N M U E A A U M N
A I U N E U G A I D N I X B N S I H A A
R N L A T T D N A L R E Z T I W S T L W
A G G L A S A I A R M E N I A Q S I A S
G A A N U H R K A B O L I V I A U L Y T
U P R I G A E R O K H T U O S R R E S O
A O I F Q B R U N E I K I R I B A T I B
Y R A T L A R B I G I T N O O R E M A C
K E N Y A G M O N G O L I A D U M R E B
C H I N A I P O I H T E R A M N A Y M A
```

AFGHANISTAN	COLOMBIA	MALAYSIA
ALGERIA	EGYPT	MONGOLIA
ANTIGUA	ETHIOPIA	MOZAMBIQUE
ARGENTINA	FINLAND	MYANMAR
ARMENIA	FRANCE	NICARAGUA
AUSTRALIA	GIBRALTAR	PAKISTAN
BANGLADESH	GREENLAND	PARAGUAY
BELARUS	GUATEMALA	PERU
BELIZE	INDIA	PORTUGAL
BERMUDA	INDONESIA	RUSSIA
BHUTAN	IRAN	SINGAPORE
BOLIVIA	IRAQ	SOMALIA
BOTSWANA	JERSEY	SOUTH KOREA
BRUNEI	KAZAKHSTAN	SPAIN
BULGARIA	KENYA	SURINAME
BURKINA FASO	KIRIBATI	SWAZILAND
CAMBODIA	KYRGYZSTAN	SWITZERLAND
CAMEROON	LITHUANIA	SYRIA
CHILE	LUXEMBOURG	THAILAND
CHINA	MADAGASCAR	URUGUAY

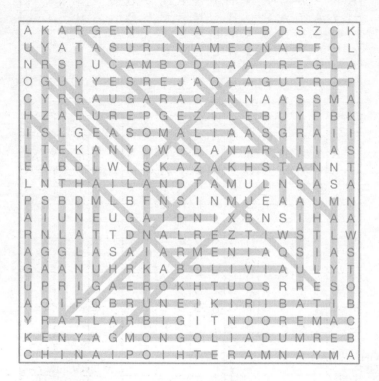

KAKURO

Instructions

Place a digit from 1 to 9 into each white square. Each
horizontal run of white squares must add up to the total
above the diagonal line to the left of the run, and each
vertical run of white squares must add up to the total
below the diagonal line above the run. **No digit can be
used more than once in any run.**

Solved example

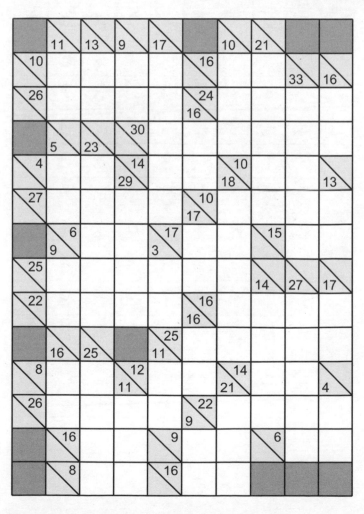

	11\	13\	9\	17\	■	10\	21\	■	■
\10	3	4	2	1	16\	7	9	33\	16\
\26	8	9	7	2	24\16	2	6	9	7
■	5\	23\	30\	3	7	1	2	8	9
\4	1	3	14\29	5	9	10\18	3	7	13\
\27	4	8	9	6	10\17	2	1	3	4
■	6\9	1	5	17\3	9	8	15\	6	9
\25	3	4	7	2	8	1	14\	27\	17\
\22	6	7	8	1	16\16	4	2	1	9
■	16\	25\	■	25\11	9	3	1	4	8
\8	7	1	12\11	5	7	14\21	5	9	4\
\26	9	8	3	6	22\9	5	6	8	3
■	16\	9	7	9\	2	7	6\	5	1
■	8\	7	1	16\	7	9	■	■	■

MIXED PUZZLES

Which of these substances is the odd one out, and why?
Carbon   **Hydrogen**   **Helium**   **Bronze**   **Copper**

Which number comes next in this sequence?
1   10   11   100   101   ____

Which of these words is the odd one out, and why?
Run   Skip   Walk   Roll   Jog

Which of these numbers is the odd one out?
351   423   711   262   180

How many seconds are there in exactly half a week?

If the Cambridge to London express train leaves Cambridge at 10:30 am and travels an average of 90 mph, while the slower non-express train for the same route leaves at 10:15 am but travels at an average of 60 mph, how many minutes sooner will the express train arrive in London, given that the distance travelled is 60 miles?

If global warming causes the height of the oceans to rise by 1cm for every half a degree Celsius rise in average temperature, and if in 40 years the temperature has risen an average of 5 Celsius then by how much will the oceans have risen?

Complete the following:
123 + 456 + 789 = ____   963 x 3 = ____   145 x 5 = ____

Which letter comes next in this pattern:
J F M A M J J ____

Complete the following:
80% of 120 = ____   2 x 58275 x 0.5 = ____   78% of 100% of 200 = ____

If I have just four matching pairs of gloves in a drawer, how many gloves do I need to pull out of the drawer to be sure of having two matching pairs?

If I toss a coin six times, what is the probability that I get six 'tail's?

I'm feeling lucky so I bet £50 on 'red' at a casino. Given that there are the numbers 0 to 36 on the board, of which 18 are red, am I more or less or equally likely to win my bet than to guess the result of a single coin toss?

Which of these substances is the odd one out, and why?
Bronze – the only one that isn't an element in the Periodic Table

Which number comes next in this sequence?
110 – it is 1, 2, 3, 4, 5, 6 in binary (base 2)

Which of these words is the odd one out, and why?
Roll – the only one that doesn't always involve using your legs to move

Which of these numbers is the odd one out?
262 – the only one whose digits don't sum to 9

How many seconds are there in exactly half a week?
302,400 seconds

If the Cambridge to London express train leaves Cambridge at 10:30 am and travels an average of 90 mph, while the slower non-express train for the same route leaves at 10:15 am but travels at an average of 60 mph, how many minutes sooner will the express train arrive in London, given that the distance travelled is 60 miles?
The express train arrives 5 minutes sooner – it takes 40 minutes and arrives at 11:10 am; the other takes an hour and arrives at 11:15 am

If global warming causes the height of the oceans to rise by 1cm for every half a degree Celsius rise in average temperature, and if in 40 years the temperature has risen an average of 5 Celsius then by how much will the oceans have risen? **10cm**

Complete the following:
123 + 456 + 789 = **1368**   963 x 3 = **2889**   145 x 5 = **725**

Which letter comes next in this pattern?
A – the first letters of the months of the year: January, February, etc

Complete the following:
80% of 120 = **96**   2 x 58275 x 0.5 = **58275**   78% of 100% of 200 = **156**

If I have just four matching pairs of gloves in a drawer, how many gloves do I need to pull out of the drawer to be sure of having two matching pairs? **6**

If I toss a coin six times, what is the probability that I get six 'tail's?
1 in 64 – 1 in 2 multiplied by itself six times

I'm feeling lucky so I bet £50 on 'red' at a casino. Given that there are the numbers 0 to 36 on the board, of which 18 are red, am I more or less or equally likely to win my bet than to guess the result of a single coin toss?
I'm less likely to win – there are 37 numbers on the board so my 18 in 37 chance is less than 1 in 2, the chance of predicting a coin toss